The Leadership House

A Leadership Tale about the Challenging Path to
Becoming an Effective Leader

PATRICK FLESNER

Registered Offices
John Wiley & Sons, Inc., 111 River Street, Hoboken, NJ 07030, USA
John Wiley & Sons Ltd, The Atrium, Southern Gate, Chichester, West Sussex, PO19 8SQ, UK

Editorial Office
The Atrium, Southern Gate, Chichester, West Sussex, PO19 8SQ, UK

For details of our global editorial offices, customer services, and more information about Wiley products visit us at www.wiley.com.

Library of Congress Cataloging-in-Publication Data is Available:

ISBN 9781394191130 (Hardback)
ISBN 9781394207077 (ePDF)
ISBN 9781394207060 (ePUB)

Cover Design: Wiley
Cover Image: © peshkov/Getty Images

Set in 12/21 pt D-DIN Condensed by Straive, Chennai, India
Printed and bound by CPI Group (UK) Ltd, Croydon, CR0 4YY

C9781394191130_160323

Praise for *The Leadership House*

"A wonderful story about leadership. In this little book you will find the tools necessary to enhance your leadership journey. Thanks, Patrick, for giving us such a gift."

—Howard Behar, former President of Starbucks International

"Patrick Flesner addresses the dimensions of leadership in a very situational and realistic manner. This book is a powerful guide for becoming aware of your own leadership skills and development potential."

—Oliver Kaltner, former CEO of Leica Camera AG

"Most leadership books are either too theoretic, esoteric, or complex—or all of the above. The Leadership House *stands out. It conveys how to lead effectively, wrapped in an inspiring story full of leadership wisdom and actionable insights. This book is not only fun to read, but makes you learn how to lead with ease. Highly recommended for any leader and all who wish to become one."*

—Matthias Heutger, Senior Vice President, Global Head of Innovation & Commercial Development at DHL Group

Also from the author:

FASTSCALING: THE SMART PATH TO BUILDING
MASSIVELY VALUABLE BUSINESSES

TO MY LONG-STANDING FRIENDS:

NINA
ARNE
CARSTEN
HENNING
JASPER
JENS-PETER
JÖRG
JÖRG-PETER
MARKUS
MATTHIAS
SEBASTIAN
TIM
TOBIAS

LET'S STAY YOUNG.
LET'S CONTINUE TO HAVE CRAZY IDEAS.
THEY HAVE ALWAYS MADE THE BEST MEMORIES.

● ● ●

I've been working in private equity, venture capital, and mergers & acquisitions for almost two decades. I've been a partner of an investment fund investing into high-growth businesses. I've been a partner of renowned business law firms. I've worked as a senior executive in a publicly traded company. I've had the pleasure of working for strong and highly effective leaders who've become role models. And I've also worked for weak leaders who taught me how not to lead. I've long been reading leadership books, attending leadership courses, and writing about leadership topics in renowned magazines like *MIT Sloan Management Review, I by IMD,* and the *Inc.* magazine. All my leadership experiences—both good and bad—have made me the leader I am today.

Throughout the years, I've translated my leadership learnings into leadership frameworks, which has helped me to lead my teams effectively while becoming a better leader every day. As an investor, startup board member, coach, and mentor, I've been passing on these leadership frameworks to founders, entrepreneurs, managers, and leaders across the globe. The feedback has been overwhelming and has compelled me to share my leadership knowledge within these pages.

While there are many books out there on the same topic, the feedback I've been receiving led me to conclude that a specific kind of leadership handbook was missing: a leadership book that provides actionable insights and frameworks people can systematically follow to develop their leadership skills, climb the leadership ladder, and lead effectively. I've closed this gap by writing this leadership tale.

Wherever you are on your particular walk of life, in your career, and in your organization, I know that you'll benefit from and find value in this leadership story. Whether you want to make the leap from founder to leader, from manager to leader, or from leader to highly effective leader, this book is for you!

Patrick Flesner

• • •

CONTENTS

Foreword

After 40 years in business—and more than 20 of those years as CEO—I have often asked myself what leadership actually means. What makes a good leader? Is there an ideal role model to follow? Which skills do you need to have, and in what intensity and composition, in order to be successful? Like many others, I've read countless business books on the subject, although to be honest, I'm not sure if they really got me anywhere. While reading them, I often tried to suit the recommendations to myself. Sometimes with success, but most often not; they just didn't align with me. I generally forgot much of the content, usually because I found it to be irrelevant. But this is also because I often had to struggle through all the recommendations, especially when they were written in a lengthy, stodgy format. However, there are some books that stand out, mostly because they were enhanced by little, poignant stories. In one of the most famous management books from 1982, called *In Search of Excellence* by Thomas J. Peters and Robert H. Waterman Jr., there was a compelling description of the author's nightly check-in at one of the most successful worldwide hotel chains. Something like that sticks, but a long, boring series of facts often doesn't. With instructional books, it's the personal touches that make the information stand out, or at least that's been my experience as a reader.

As a CEO, however, you're less of a receiver and more of a sender in terms of information. You give many speeches and you often have to deal with the media and investors. Here's what I know about delivering a message: if you only line up the facts, people will eventually stop listening to you, and they will probably forget a lot of what you are saying (sometimes immediately). But if you throw in a great story here and there, it becomes a different experience. Suddenly, everyone is back in the game. Sometimes, they're even captivated with your message.

But storytelling should also not be too trivial. If you tell one tale after the other, people stop listening after a while. But great storytelling alongside the simultaneous communication of facts is the silver bullet. And this is the case with Patrick's leadership book. The essentials of leadership are impressively presented in an unusual and memorable setting. I don't want to give anything away. All I'll say is that it's the personal touches that matter. It's the personal touches that teach. This book has that personal touch.

Enjoy the ride.

—Gisbert Rühl, former CEO of Klöckner & Co SE

Introduction

Whether you're a CEO, a founder, an entrepreneur, or have just been promoted into a leadership position, your success will always depend on others. If you cannot lead people, groups, and organizations effectively, your teams will fail—and *you* will fail as a leader. It's as simple as that. In contrast, if you understand how to inspire your teams, how to figure out what intrinsically motivates your team members, and how to transform a set of strong individuals into a thriving, cohesive team, the sky is the limit. If you know how to lead effectively and are at ease with your leadership role, you can achieve the extraordinary.

But if you're like many of the founders, entrepreneurs, and managers I worked with or interviewed for this book, you'll agree that becoming an effective leader is a daunting task. It's difficult because the leadership advice we get is often fragmented. We read that we're supposed to inspire, trust, and empower. We hear that the best leaders show their vulnerability, that they're humble and strong at the same time. We're advised not to micromanage. In doing all of these things, we shall lead our team members and turn our followers into leaders. While all this may be true and is actually great advice, it's not *consolidated* advice. Leadership advice comes in a piecemeal fashion, which is frustrating. As soon as we're back in the trenches, we feel overwhelmed and don't know which theory to apply. Should we get our hands dirty and show our teams how to do it? Or are we better off assuming a coaching role and guiding our teams by asking great questions to help them find the answers themselves?

If you are even slightly like the leaders I've been working with throughout the last two decades, you want to lead systematically. But eventually, you end up *only* following your gut feeling. The goal of this book is to provide you with the system you've been searching for.

The Leadership House framework and the additional frameworks I'll be sharing with you throughout this tale have helped many leaders before you. I am convinced that they'll also help you to systematically develop your leadership skills and transform you into a leader who leads with ease.

There is, however, one important caveat. While this book contains many leadership frameworks you can apply in your leadership role, you must never forget that *leadership is a privilege*.

You are not a leader because of the frameworks you apply. You are not a leader because of your title or role. You are a leader because of the teams who want to be led by you. Leadership roles are something to be earned—they are rarely just given to us. Let's remember this as we continue to lead and inspire our teams into success and greatness.

The Tale

REFUSAL

"The future rewards those who press on. I don't have time to feel sorry for myself. I don't have time to complain. I am going to press on."

—Barack Obama

"I'm sorry, Felix, but tomorrow will be your last day as the CEO of our company."

"But Peter..."

"My apologies—I have to jump on another call. See you tomorrow." With that, Peter ended the call, leaving a baffled Felix to wonder what on earth had just happened.

Felix set the phone down and slumped into a chair at the conference room table. The room was characterized by a minimalist design style: six designer office chairs upholstered with white leather surrounded a rectangular, bright white, enamel conference table. On the wall, a two-square-meter photograph of a calm ocean wave conveyed a sense of mindfulness. Felix liked this minimalist design style; it conveyed to him both luxury and simplicity. Similar high-end styles could only be found in the startup's other conference rooms and in the two founders' offices.

Peter Sting, who had just informed Felix that his time as CEO was up, was the founding partner of Sting Investment Partners. The famous American venture capital firm had invested twenty million into the company that Felix and his co-founder Mark had founded six years ago.

Slowly, Felix put his iPhone back into the pocket of his black G-Star jeans. He felt cold sweat creeping down his back underneath his white, collared shirt. Paralyzed, he whispered to himself, "This can't be true. This *can't* be true."

His co-founder, who'd been privy to the brief exchange, pressed him to know what had just occurred. "What did he say? Felix, what did he say?"

"He said he'd finally convinced Douglas that I'm a bad leader," Felix stammered. "That I'm unable to grow the business any further... that I'm the wrong person in the driver's seat and that I have to be removed from office. Then he said he wants us to hold an extraordinary board meeting tomorrow at noon—he and Douglas will come to our office so that all board members can participate in person. They really want to fire me this time, Mark."

"Really?" Mark asked.

"Yes. This is actually happening."

"But that's not fair, Felix! This is our company. We founded it. I mean, yes, Douglas is the one who invested five hundred thousand when we'd first started out with just an idea. And Peter wrote a big check three years ago. All that's true. But we're holding the majority of the shares in our company. And those guys are just two out of four members of the board of directors. The board is in charge of supervising and advising the management team, but..."

"And the board can fire us, Mark," Felix interrupted with a defeated sigh. "That's what we finally agreed on when Peter invested. We agreed that the board could fire us if two out of four board members believed it was the best choice for the company. I never thought they'd make use of that power, but it seems that our business angel and our venture capital investor are doing it. They're doing it right now."

"What about me? Will I be fired, too?"

"I don't know, Mark. But I don't think so. I mean, Peter only blamed *me* for the situation we're in. He didn't say anything about you."

Felix gazed through the glass panes of the conference room and into the open office space. Employees were working and carrying on as if nothing unusual had happened. They certainly didn't know that Felix was about to be fired; the day simply carried on as usual as his career sat on the chopping block. He thoughtfully turned to Mark and said, "Isn't this crazy? Six years ago, we started this company. Since then, we grew sales from nothing to fifteen million, expanded from Germany to Spain, Italy, France, and the UK, gave jobs to more than two hundred people, moved into this fancy office... and now they're firing me."

"We've fought similar battles before, Felix," Mark replied. "Let's fight again. Let's roll up our sleeves and find a way out." As both Felix and Mark used to wear their shirt sleeves rolled up all the time, they usually laughed whenever Mark said this. But Felix was in no mood for jokes.

"I don't know, Mark. Yes, we've fought many battles. But I'm getting tired of these fights with Peter. I'm fed up of hearing that I'm not leading this business effectively, that I'm not growing the business as promised, that the office is too expensive, that I'm generally not frugal enough, that we're burning too much cash, that I'm not transparent with the board, and all the other accusations. Maybe the time has come for me to let go."

"It's not the first time Peter's questioned your leadership skills and has threatened to fire you," Mark reminded Felix.

"That's true. But this is the first time he could convince Douglas to join forces with him. It's the first time both Douglas and Peter seem to agree that I'm a bad leader. I'm tired, Mark."

"Don't give up, Felix! Why don't you give Douglas a call and convince him that you deserve another chance?"

"No—not again. Douglas has helped me so many times when Peter wanted me to leave. If he's switched sides now, so be it."

"But what are you planning on doing if you're not our CEO anymore? We've invested all our money into this company. Do you want to work in your family's business? Do you want to work for your father?"

"That's the last thing I'm going to do, Mark. Begging my father for a job and admitting that I failed? No way. He always said I was stupid to found a startup."

"Felix, let's fight!"

"Not this time. Let's call it a day, Mark," Felix said, struggling to his feet and heading for the door.

"You can't just leave, Felix. This is also *my* company. You leaving affects me, too. Why don't we assemble the entire leadership team and come up with a solution?"

"We're not going to tell anybody about this, Mark. We've always kept these kinds of topics between the two of us—just you and me. And this is exactly what we'll be doing this time."

"But this is nothing to be ashamed of, Felix! Being a leader is difficult. We can all improve."

"What are you saying, Mark? Do you think I'm a bad leader, too?"

"No, no... I mean... I just mean we *all* can improve, can't we? Maybe Douglas will change his mind if you promise to work on your leadership skills and if we can come up with a new growth plan."

Felix had heard enough. "Thanks, Mark!" he said with a sarcastic smile. "This was the last thing I needed. After six years of working together, my co-founder is telling me that I'm a bad leader. I've done my very best, Mark. We are where we are because of the market environment that turned difficult during COVID-19.

Have you forgotten how many of our business customers didn't make it through the pandemic? And we are where we are because many of our best hires haven't been living up to our expectations. I do *not* believe that our situation has anything to do with me and my leadership skills. See you tomorrow, Mark." Felix swung open the door and stormed out of the conference room.

On his way to the staircase, he heard one last plea from Mark: "Don't go, Felix! It's my company, too! Don't let me down! Let's give it another try!"

But Felix did not go back. He exhaustedly forged down the stairs, passed through the entrance hall, and left the office building in a flurry of frustration, disappointment, and anger. "I'm so tired of being challenged as a leader," he thought. "This is the last time somebody questions my leadership skills—at least until our board meeting tomorrow."

He had no idea just how wrong that sentiment was.

AN UNEXPECTED MEETING

"Rapport is the ultimate tool for producing results with other people. No matter what you want in your life, if you can develop rapport with the right people, you'll be able to fill their needs, and they will be able to fill yours."

—Tony Robbins

I t was mid-September and still about twenty degrees Celsius at six in the evening. Not entirely unusual for Cologne, but much cooler weather would be on its way soon, for certain. Felix stood in front of the office building, his face looking skyward; the sun felt refreshing after such a stifled, frustrating experience back upstairs. "Crazy that there are still people out there denying climate change and global warming," he thought. His thoughts were happy to wander for a moment. He hadn't a clue what to do with himself—or what to think. His mind was still reeling.

The office building was in a former media park. The park had been fully renovated with public money in 2012 after almost the entire media industry had moved from Cologne to Berlin. The Ministry of Economy, which had funded the renovation project, wanted to create a new tech hub in the heart of Cologne.

This tech ecosystem was supposed to attract innovative startups and founders who didn't want to live and work in Berlin or Munich, the cities where the German startup scene prevailed.

The area that had been the media park suited this plan perfectly. It was easily accessible; the subway to the main train station was nearby, as was the complete infrastructure for work and leisure. Five office towers with five floors each provided enough space for a startup ecosystem to develop. The offices in all five towers provided maximum flexibility. There were suitable room solutions for every challenge: big rooms with moveable walls that enabled startups to adapt the rooms to their specific needs, smaller rooms that were used as conference rooms, and spacious work lofts that became open offices with small cubicles in which employees could make phone or video calls.

The office towers were especially famous for their spectacular rooftop terraces, which offered a fantastic view across Cologne. At ground floor, there were all kinds of amenities that you'd find in *WeWork*-type spaces: lounge corners, coffee tables, and even a bar where employees could get drinks and snacks. If employees wanted to have lunch or dinner, they'd find hip restaurants all around the media park area. The whole renovation project was a big success, and it didn't take long until the offices were squatted by startups and founders who wanted to create the next big thing—a company worth more than a billion and what the industry calls a "unicorn."

Before Felix's company had rented the entire fifth floor of the middle office tower, he'd rented some desks and a team office at an incubator in the office tower to the left.

In addition to desks and team offices, the incubator offered all startups advice, coaching, workshops, and events, as well as connections to a large network of startup service providers and investors. Every Thursday evening, the incubator organized an event for all tenants and the wider incubator network. These events were often fireside chats between the incubator CEO and interesting guests from the startup ecosystem. Other times, they were pitching events where founders pitched their business ideas to potential investors. And, occasionally, the incubator CEO would also attract renowned business angels and investors to give a keynote speech followed by Q&A and a networking session with a barbecue and free drinks. Felix especially liked the keynote speeches and actively engaged in the Q&A sessions. He felt he learnt a lot from these very experienced investors who shared their best practices, actionable insights, and useful frameworks.

Thinking about the good old times and all those fantastic events, Felix suddenly remembered he'd been invited to an event today, too. This time, the incubator CEO had made a big buzz around the event and the business angel who was scheduled to talk. The incubator CEO hadn't even shared the business angel's name, but stressed in his newsletter email that one of the most successful and famous business angels would be giving a keynote speech about 'leadership and growth' that evening. Q&A, a barbecue, and free drinks would follow.

"Why not go there and listen to this famous guy, get some distraction, and have some beers afterwards?" Felix thought, looking at his watch. Unlike other founders, Felix didn't wear an Apple watch, but rather a Maurice Lacroix chronograph he'd inherited from his grandfather. Felix had had a very close relationship with his grandfather, his mentor, before he passed away eight years ago. He'd always admired his grandfather, especially for his entrepreneurial spirit that had enabled him to found the family business more than sixty years ago. His grandfather had become an entrepreneur at the young age of twenty.

Felix saw on his Lacroix that it was 6:10 p.m. The event was scheduled for 6:15. He realized he could still make it in time if he hurried. Not wasting any time, he turned to the left and walked rapidly towards the next office tower.

Just a few moments later, he entered the hallway of the nearby building at Media Park 5. Different from the hallways in most other office towers, this one was kept simple. No fancy coffee bars. No nice parquet floor. Just a clean hallway with a dark, shiny stone floor, with the stairway to the left and the elevator to the right. Felix remembered the story around this building—everyone said that it hadn't been completely renovated for legal reasons, but nobody really knew what those reasons were. He always favored taking the stairs whenever possible; elevators made him claustrophobic. But as he turned towards the stairway, he noticed a sign saying 'Wet Paint! Please Take the Elevator!' A bit disappointed, he hesitantly walked to the elevator and pressed the button. A loud, almost ancient bell signaled that the elevator was set in motion. Felix looked up and saw the lights denoting the floor numbers the elevator was slowly, slowly passing. *5... 4... 3...*

"Good Lord—this elevator looks prehistoric," he thought, just as the elevator finally arrived. The dark red sliding doors opened loudly. Felix entered the cabin and immediately noticed the *No Smoking* sign that decorated the brown plastic back wall of the cabin. "Nice brown," Felix said aloud to himself sarcastically. He turned to the metallic panel sheet and pressed the button for the fifth floor. The buttons, obviously white once upon a time, were now stained yellow. "Ridiculous," Felix huffed. "People must have still smoked in elevators when this thing was built." He smushed the dirty-looking button into the panel and the door began to close with the same mechanical noise it screeched on opening.

Suddenly, Felix heard a female voice shouting from the hallway, "Stop, stop— please wait!" He held his hand between the elevator doors and thanked God the elevator had been equipped with a safety light barrier. "Losing my hand would have been the perfect end to this damn day," Felix said to himself after the door opened. A woman entered the cabin and, almost out of breath, thanked Felix for waiting for her.

"No problem," he responded, catching the soft scent of her light, floral perfume as the door shut. As she turned to him, he couldn't believe his eyes. Was this Uma Thurman, the actress who'd become famous for her appearances in Quentin Tarantino movies? It couldn't be, but he was shocked at the resemblance.

Similar face with a similarly sleepy look. Bright blue eyes. Long blond hair, a bit curly, falling onto a black leather jacket over a long white shirt. Its upper buttons open, the shirt revealed a niggle of a white bra. "Not too much skin, and not too little. Cool style," Felix thought, covertly eyeballing every inch of Thurman's very convincing doppelganger. The black leather pants and black high heels made the whole outfit perfect. She must have been in her fifties—she had an older air about her—but the way she was put together made her look more like a woman who'd just turned forty.

"I know," she said to Felix, clearly noticing his gaze. "I look a bit like her, but I am *not* her."

Feeling caught for examining her a little too closely, Felix stammered, "Oh, I'm sorry, it's just that..."

"You did not expect to meet Uma Thurman in an elevator today? No need to be sorry. People think I am her all the time."

Felix noticed that she spoke in a light yet formal manner and didn't really use contractions; she seemed to favor "I am" instead of "I'm," and so forth. He found it endearing, laughed a bit nervously, then politely asked, "Which floor?"

"Fifth, please."

"Oh, are you sure? There's a startup event on that floor tonight."

"Should I *not* be going to a startup event?"

"No, of course you should, but…"

"I do not look like someone who attends startup events?"

"No, of course you do. I mean…" Felix smiled sheepishly. "Well, I've already pressed the correct button then."

The elevator moved up from the ground floor like an old steamer. First floor, second floor, third floor… Suddenly, the lights in the elevator flickered and it came to an abrupt, noisy halt, sounding as if two cars had crashed into each other.

"No, no, no," Felix moaned. "We're not actually stuck in an elevator, are we?"

"Seems like," the woman responded. "I guess it must happen pretty often to an antique lift like this." She looked at her phone and said, "No connectivity. Should we press the alarm button?"

Felix nodded and turned to the panel, pressing the red button that would signal distress in the elevator. No sound. He pressed again… and again. But the sound they both expected never came to pierce the awkward silence. "Well, this is fitting—what an absolutely perfect day," Felix said, laughing and groaning at the same time.

Do not worry. Maybe It is only us who cannot hear the alarm. I would think there is definitely someone somewhere who is being informed that we are stuck. And the event organizer might also notice we are missing. Hopefully he will figure out we are stuck in this relict from the last century."

"I hope so. Although I guess the organizer's used to people signing up but not showing. And I didn't even sign up for this event," Felix said. "Did you?"

"Yes. I guess they will notice I am missing."

"Sure. They will…" Felix began to breathe a bit heavily. "To be honest, I don't deal very well with small rooms—I'm a bit claustrophobic."

"Oh, no. Well, just try and stay calm. Everything will be all right. They will solve this problem really soon, and then we will be out of here. Is there anything I can do?"

Felix breathed in and out slowly, eventually calming down. "No, I'll be fine. But thank you."

 "Well, let's just chat a bit, then—it will help you forget all about the situation. Shall we introduce ourselves?

"I'm Miss Mia Wallace."

"Not funny," Felix said, but with a smile. "I know who Miss Mia Wallace is. Uma Thurman played Mia Wallace in *Pulp Fiction*, and I love that movie. I actually love almost all Tarantino movies."

"You caught me. Actually, I am Sophia. I love the movie, too. And I am also a big Tarantino fan. I even bought myself the yellow Triumph motorcycle Uma Thurman rides in *Kill Bill*. I am loving it. What is your name?"

"I'm Felix. Nice to meet you. Even under these weird circumstances."

"Indeed—I know cozier places," she said with a bit of a grin. "So, I am Sophia, Sophia van de Sand. I am the CEO of a Dutch family business. You may have heard of Sand Enterprises. Not as big a company as Heineken, but decently sized. I am here to attend the incubator event. I like today's topic a lot—'Leadership and Growth'. I believe many companies fail to grow their businesses because their leaders fail to become effective. I am looking forward to hearing what everybody else thinks in this regard."

"Christ, enough of this leadership stuff. I've had enough of hearing about that today," Felix thought, but then replied, "I'm also a CEO. I'm the founder and CEO of a company called Digitally. The company name is written as DGTLY. I founded the company when I was in university six years ago."

"How old are you, if I may?"

"Twenty-eight."

"Wow—that is great, Felix. I mean, not that you are twenty-eight, but that you founded a business at the age of twenty-two. I admire people like you—people who embark on these challenging founder journeys, especially at that age. Why not give me your elevator pitch?"

Felix laughed at the irony and said, "I've never given an elevator pitch inside an elevator before. The fact that the elevator isn't moving... does that mean I have more time than I would ordinarily for this pitch?"

"Nope," Sophia said, playfully crossing her arms. "You should be able to explain to me what your company does and wants to achieve in a pitch that does not take longer than a typical elevator ride. If you cannot explain it simply, then you do not understand it well enough, as Albert Einstein said. You should be able to pitch me your company in no more than thirty seconds."

Felix paused, looked at Sophia, and thought, "Weird—sometimes there are people that we never click with, even over years, try as we might. And other times, we get along so well with people we've only known for mere moments." He felt the latter about Sophia—an instant connection.

"Why not?" Felix thought, shrugging. "One more elevator pitch won't make a difference."

But every pitch can.

THE LEADERSHIP DRAMA TRIANGLE

"The leaders who work most effectively, it seems to me, never say 'I'. And that's not because they have trained themselves not to say 'I'. They don't think 'I'. They think 'we'; they think 'team'. They understand their job to be to make the team function. They accept responsibility and don't sidestep it, but 'we' gets the credit."

—Peter Drucker

"Okay, Sophia. We've got nothing else to do in here, so here's my elevator pitch." Felix brushed his fingers through his blond hair. He immediately took on a professional stance; he knew that proper posture is of critical importance for a great pitch, and that body language, when properly used, could be a key to greater success. Felix stood tall and took up some extra space to nonverbally display confidence; he knew all the tricks. He widened his stance, relaxed his knees, centered his weight in his lower body, and held his arms at waist level. His green eyes looked into Sophia's. Then, with an open-armed gesture displaying the palms of his hands, he began.

"I'm Felix. I'm the founder of Digitally—written as DGTLY. In 2016, I founded DGTLY with the vision of enabling small- and medium-sized businesses to use the same digital tools big enterprises use and can afford. The goal has always been to make small- and medium-sized businesses, especially restaurants, more efficient. I started out selling digital tools that our customers could use to better forecast their cashflows. You know, many small- and medium-sized businesses close shop because they cannot manage their cashflows properly and run out of cash. Our tools are all digital and can be integrated into the most relevant other systems. They can be integrated into the most popular cashier systems, in order to get accurate data on revenues. And they can be integrated into all cost-relevant systems like ERP and HR systems. With this understanding in terms of how revenues and costs usually develop, our tools can accurately forecast our customers' cashflows. Meanwhile, I'm also selling to enterprise clients. And I've also broadened our solution portfolio, offering a magnitude of digital tools that help our customers improve. For instance, we offer scheduling, payrolling, and absence management tools that save our customers a lot of time and help them increase revenues and reduce costs. Last year, the company generated more than fifteen million in revenue, selling to more than ten thousand customers in Germany, the UK, France, Spain, and Italy. I've been backed by business angel Douglas Kent and Sting Capital Investment Partners. Sting is quite a famous US venture capital firm—they invested twenty million in our last financing round back in 2019. I'm currently looking for a growth capital investor willing to invest in us to further fuel our growth. Looking forward to hearing what you think, Sophia."

Sophia paused a moment, and then said to Felix, "A lot of *I*, isn't there?"

He was a bit stunned. "That's all? I've given you my pitch in this elevator and your only comment is, 'A lot of *I*? What do you mean, 'A lot of *I*?"

"I mean exactly what I have said." She smiled confidently. "Not more, not less. You have used a lot of *I* in your pitch."

"And?" Felix asked, slightly irritated. "What's the problem?"

"Well, Felix, I offered to listen to your pitch mainly as a way to pass the time. But if you are open to feedback, I am happy to give you some."

"I usually get feedback about the business and not about how many times I use *I*. But please go ahead. It doesn't matter anymore anyway."

"Sure. It is great that you are open to feedback. Not every leader is. Listen, Felix. You have strong presentation skills—no doubt about that. Good body language. And you maintained eye contact throughout the pitch. I understand what you are doing and why your customers need your products and services. It would not have hurt if you had told me a bit more about the size of the market and a bit more about your growth plans. If the market is small or shrinking, you will never be able to create a big business. Market size and market dynamics are always very important to me. But you had only thirty seconds. And an elevator pitch is no more than just a teaser. It is supposed to create appetite for learning more about your business. We can still discuss market sizing and growth plans in more detail."

"It's a huge market. And it's growing."

"That is what all founders say," she said with a smirk. "But, in fact, most markets are smaller than founders think they are. In your case, I also think it is a big market, but this would have to be confirmed. I was a bit surprised to hear that you have started selling to enterprise customers, too. I thought you mentioned they could already afford to use other tools. At a later stage, I would be interested in understanding what you had in mind when you decided to go after this additional customer segment. And how this move fits into your vision to digitize small- and medium-sized businesses. But, again, you only had thirty seconds. You cannot cover everything in thirty seconds. However, most importantly, you have given me the impression that it has been only *you*. You have given me the impression that you *alone* have achieved all this. Have you ever heard the saying, 'There is no *I* in *team*'? I would imagine you have *not* done all this on your own, have you?"

"Of course not. I've got a co-founder. His name's Mark. And certainly, I—sorry, *we*—also have a very strong leadership team and great employees."

"I am happy to hear this, Felix. When I listen to pitches, I normally concentrate on two things: I want to understand the market opportunity, and I want to understand whether the leader is strong and has built a strong team. I am an absolute believer in the power of teams and teamwork. A good team will succeed in any market. A bad team will fail, irrespective of how good the market opportunity, the idea, or the business is. In my view, it is ultimately all about leadership. Strong, effective leaders build strong leadership teams. And these teams succeed. So, what could be wrong with your team?"

"Nothing is wrong," he said defensively "Why do you think anything is wrong?"

"I am not judging. I do not know if something is wrong with your team. But you said, 'It doesn't matter anymore anyway.' This has sounded a bit as if something was wrong."

"Oh. *That.* You're a good listener. No, that didn't mean anything."

"Ah, I see. So, you have found a new growth capital investor willing to invest in you?"

"No, not yet."

"What is the reason for that?"

"As a CEO of a family business, you may not be familiar with the venture capital industry and the fundraising process. But as a founder, you've got to kiss many frogs until you find your prince. Raising money from investors takes time."

"Ah, sure. When did you start with your fundraising?"

"End of last year."

"End of last year?"

"Yes. As I said, fundraising takes time."

"Sure. I understand. But what has been the response from the potential investors you have been pitching to the last nine months?" she asked him.

"That we do not meet their specific investment criteria. Some said it was too early and that we had to generate more revenue first. Others said it was too late for them, as they focused on investing in very early-stage businesses. Wrong industry. Wrong business model. Many different reasons. But many did say they were interested, want to stay in touch, and want to look into the next financing round."

"They want to look into the next financing round? Isn't this a typical response you get from almost all investors? I have heard VCs rarely completely turn down investment opportunities. They want to keep their options open. But maybe it is just a stereotype and not true at all."

"As soon as we meet their investment requirements, they'll invest. Believe me!"

"Sure," Sophia smiled. "I am happy that everything is fine and that you are on a successful growth journey. I have heard that many startups fail to get from initial traction to sustainable high growth, and that many founders struggle making the leap from founder to leader. But if you do not have any problem, then there is no value-add I can provide."

Silence.

Then Sophia added, "Felix, it is all good. You do not have to share any details with me. I just have this kind of feeling that your situation is not as good as you try to convey. Nine months strikes me as a pretty long time to be fundraising. And the fundraising has not even been successful until now. If I can believe what people say, then the best startups complete their funding rounds after one to three months. And you certainly do not have to share any details with me. But if you were interested in candid feedback and maybe some helpful thoughts from my side, you would have to be transparent and share with me the problems you are facing, if any. Otherwise, I cannot help you. As I am also a CEO, I know that I have to treat any information you share with me confidentially. But it is up to you."

Felix did not know why, but somehow, he felt that Sophia was trustworthy and could share some interesting insights. She wasn't from the venture capital world, but maybe this was actually a good thing. And what difference would it make anyway? Tomorrow, he would be without a job. "Okay, Sophia. You're right. It's not all roses and sunshine like I made it sound. We've been trying to raise some twenty million for more than nine months. And we've only received 'no's so far. The main feedback has been that we haven't been growing enough since our last financing round, and that we've been burning too much cash at the same time. And to be very honest, an hour ago, I received a call from my investor. He said I was a bad leader and that the board had decided to remove me from office tomorrow. So yeah—I guess you could say it's *not* all that shiny and perfect."

"Oh, I am sorry to hear this, Felix. Thanks for being transparent. I will certainly honor this. What is your view about your leadership skills?"

"I believe I'm a decent leader," he told her, and he meant it. "I don't think we're in this difficult state because of my leadership skills or my leadership style. We are where we are because of the market dynamics. Previously, investors poured tons of cash into startups that had not grown cash efficiently at all, but it seems that since the pandemic, investors have started focusing on profitable businesses and those that grow cash efficiently. It's just a major storm out there, as you know. Public markets have tanked. States have increased interest rates to counter inflation. Valuations of venture-backed companies have foundered. And investors have stopped investing. Also, many of our target customers have not made it through the pandemic. Many small- and medium-sized businesses had to close shop. None of that is my fault. And, by the way, the only reason we've invested so heavily in growth without thinking too much about cash burn is that our VC wanted us to scale the business this way. Peter always said, 'It's all about revenue growth, Felix. Grow, grow, grow! The rest will follow naturally.' But it hasn't worked out. We haven't been able to grow the business fast and have still burnt a lot of cash. And now they want to fire me. A bit unfair, don't you think? And our business angel did not help me much either—at least not after Peter had invested in the company. While Douglas and Peter didn't agree on many things, Peter could always succeed in the board. Eventually we did what he wanted us to do. Maybe we would have been more successful if we'd worked with this famous business angel who's currently talking upstairs. But guys like him are very hard to attract."

"What else?" Sophia asked. She was keenly interested in Felix's thoughts.

"Hmm, what else... well, I'm also quite disappointed about the work attitude some of my important hires have shown. As we hadn't been growing as expected—despite the money we had invested in growth—we hired a Chief Revenue Officer who was supposed to take care of marketing, sales, and customer success. He was expected to ignite exponential growth. But the guy left after just a few months."

"Why did he leave?"

"I don't really know. He said he didn't like the team and didn't see how he could grow the business in this setup. But this was what we hired him for, no? To make it happen. I gave him the freedom he needed. I would just let him do his business. I didn't ask questions. He had a very good resume. I was convinced he could do it. But no. He didn't pull it off."

"What else?"

"What else?" Felix was fired up now. "The Chief Revenue Officer was not the only hire who didn't live up to our expectations. For instance, there was also this country manager in charge of our UK business. He didn't pull it off at all. I explained to him how we work and what we expect from our country managers. I told him how we grow our country businesses. But all I received as a response was, 'It won't work like this', 'I disagree', and 'We have to change our go-to-market-strategy'. He just wouldn't listen, you know? He only disagreed—with everything—so I had no choice but to fire him."

"What did he say when you fired him?"

"He certainly got defensive and told me I was a bad listener and that I was bound to fail. So it's a good thing I fired him."

"Oh gosh, Felix. Have you ever heard of the *drama triangle*?"

"No, what's that?"

"The drama triangle describes the roles people usually play in critical situations, especially conflicts. There are three roles. Firstly, you have the victim."

"The victim?"

"Yes. The victim is not an *actual* victim, not like at a crime scene or anything like that. Rather, it is someone feeling or acting as if he or she cannot do anything to change the situation. The victim believes he or she tries hard, but that all attempts are futile. Victims like this role because they do not have to change, they do not have to tackle problems, and they can avoid making tough decisions. They believe they cannot change anything anyway. In all fairness, Felix, you have just played this 'poor me' role when you referred to the external circumstances your company faces. 'Funding is difficult to get because of the macroeconomic situation, and investors look for different kinds of startups— startups that are profitable or grow more cash efficiently.' Poor you! There is nothing you can do."

"No, wait a minute here..." Felix interrupted, but Sophia continued.

"Felix, please wait. Please let me finish first. The funny aspect of the drama triangle is that although it is a triangle, it does not have to be three people. People can shift roles. Let me tell you about the second role people play."

"Okay," Felix said, deciding to hear her out a little bit longer. "Go ahead."

"The second role people play is the role of the persecutor, or the villain. The villain blames others for the situation they are in. They say things like, 'This is all your fault' and 'He made this decision, not me'. You switched into the villain role when you blamed your investor, your Chief Revenue Officer, and your country manager for not having helped, for not having 'pulled it off', and for not having had the right work attitude. The beauty of being in the villain's position is that you can also neglect any responsibility and do not have to change yourself. Same as with the victim role."

Felix couldn't hold back any longer. "That's not fair. Why is it my fault if my investor demands we grow faster and doesn't care about growth efficiency? Why is it my fault if my Chief Revenue Officer throws in the towel? What can I do about a country manager who constantly underperforms?"

"Victim," Sophia said with a sympathetic, maybe even an empathetic, smile.

"Victim?"

"Yes. Victim. As I said, people can switch roles. For instance, if blamed, villains usually become defensive and assume the victim role. I am sorry, Felix, but this is what you have been doing over the last few minutes. You have been switching back and forth between the victim and the villain role."

"I don't know if I agree. But go on and humor me—what is the third role? Am I playing the third role, too?"

"The third role is that of the rescuer. You probably will not be surprised that the rescuer's role is to help. They demonstrate a 'let me help you' attitude. Victims often look for rescuers, but the role of a rescuer is dissatisfactory. If the rescuer succeeds, the victim remains a victim because he or she was unable to solve his or her problems on his or her own. The victim remains dependent on the rescuer and therefore remains a victim. And if the rescuer fails, both rescuer and victim can switch into the villain role and blame each other for having failed. To your question, Felix, I have not seen you taking on the rescuer role. But I have worked with leaders who took on the rescuer role, especially in the leader–follower situation in which the team members asked the leader for advice. While the intention of giving advice is good, doing so puts the leader who's giving the advice into the rescuer role and leaves the team member in the victim role."

"What should the leader do instead?"

"Good question. The point of the drama triangle is that there is only one good position to take."

"Which is?"

"Outside the triangle," she explained with a smile. "An effective leader avoids becoming a victim, a villain, or a rescuer. Effective leaders do not blame and do not complain. They assume full ownership of the results their teams and organizations achieve. And, in situations where team members ask for advice, effective leaders hold off on giving it. Instead, they help team members step outside the drama triangle and leave the victim role by helping them find good solutions themselves. They ask many good questions that help team members find solutions on their own. They share with their team members solutions that solved similar problems in the past. They offer to spend additional time with their team members in order to jointly work on finding solutions. They find other ways to help their team members. The point is that effective leaders are approachable and help their team members. But they avoid playing the rescuer role. They do not help in terms of having all the answers, but by coaching and guiding their team members towards solutions."

"This drama triangle theory is very interesting. But what do you suggest I do to solve my problems? Should I just neglect the market dynamics and hope my leadership team pulls it off?"

"What do you think you could do?"

"If I understand this theory correctly, I must step outside the drama triangle—now. I must not blame anyone, and I must not play the victim. Well, it's simple then. It's all my fault. That's great—it's all my fault. Sophia, this is a nice theory. And maybe it has some merits in your corporate world. But in a startup environment, life's just different. And to be honest, I don't need another person telling me I'm not a good leader. This won't help me today. Sorry, but no."

Sophia paused thoughtfully. "Felix, I embrace what I call 'the radical transparency principle'. Maybe my view is a radical one, but I strongly believe that there are no bad teams, only bad leaders. Or let me say it differently: not necessarily *bad* leaders, but *ineffective* leaders. The only way leaders like you can get out of the drama triangle is by assuming full responsibility for the situation. By not playing the blame game. And by stopping their complaining." She paused again and offered a gentle smile. "Felix, it seems we may still have some time to spend together in this malfunctioning device from the past, this broken-down elevator. If you believed my theory for just a moment, and if you believed it is *always* the leader's responsibility, we could use this time to talk a bit more about leadership. You may not like everything you hear, but why don't you give it a try?"

Felix didn't answer immediately. While he didn't like being challenged in this way, he had to admit that Sophia had made some intriguing points. He sensed that she was honest and genuinely interested in his situation. This woman was not only good looking, but also intelligent, warm, attentive, and easy to relate to. Telling himself that there could have been worse people to get stuck with in an elevator, Felix responded, "Why not? Tell me why you believe it's always the leader's fault. Let's talk about leadership. Although, to be honest, I doubt there's a lot I don't already know, save for the drama triangle.

I've been a leader for several years already."

"Have you ever heard the term 'leadership debt'?"

He hadn't.

"Well then, it seems there is still *something* you do not know yet about leadership," Sophia replied with a gentle laugh. "Let's see if you have incurred some leadership debt along your way. Fine with you?"

"Fine with me," Felix replied, curious to hear what leadership debt was.

CHAPTER 4

LEADERSHIP DEBT

"If you're struggling to recruit great people, if your investors are getting impatient because you're not filling positions quickly enough or if your early employees seem to be struggling in leadership roles, then you, my friend, probably have leadership debt."

—Martina van Hettinga

"I recently came across a research report discussing startup failures," Sophia told him. By this time, the both of them were sitting down in the elevator; they still had no idea how long they'd be stranded in there for. "According to the report, which was co-authored by researchers from Stanford and Berkeley, nine out of ten startups fail. According to another study, only less than one percent of all startups manage to generate more than ten million in revenue. Why do you think most startups fail, Felix?"

Felix smiled and replied, "They run out of cash?"

"If it only was that easy, Felix. In my humble view, running out of cash is not a *reason for* failure, but a *consequence of* failure. Why do startups run out of cash?"

"Because they've got negative cash flow. They burn too much cash. And investors don't provide them with the required financing. Investors don't invest in these companies anymore."

"And why do these investors refrain from investing in these companies?"

"Because they believe something isn't quite right," he said. "They see flaws in the business model. They don't believe in the market. They don't invest because they can't agree with the founders on the company valuation. There are thousands of reasons why investors pass on investment opportunities. This is what happened to us, too."

"Sure. Understood. And why do the businesses have all these flaws, Felix? Take, as an example, a company targeting a market that is not large enough. Why did the company go after that market?"

"Because that might have been the original idea—to solve this specific market need."

"Yes, of course. But who had the original idea?"

"The founders."

"Exactly. *The founders.*"

"But wait," Felix replied. "Sometimes it's the growth team, the marketing, or the sales team who recommend going after a specific market opportunity."

"This may be the case. But who hired and guided the people who recommended targeting this market?"

"The founders? No—that's too easy, Sophia. The founders do not, and cannot, hire everyone. There's always the HR department and other leaders who make hiring decisions."

"Who hired the first employees and who hired the people who hired the people who made bad decisions, Felix? It is the founders. If startups fail—and this applies to all kinds of companies alike, not only startups—they fail because their leaders make bad decisions. There are no bad teams, Felix. There are only bad leaders. Sorry—*ineffective* leaders."

"I'm not convinced. If you were right, it would always be the founders' fault. Isn't this a bit too easy?"

"It may sound too easy, but that is the way I see it," she said. "If you call yourself a leader and your team or organization fails, it is your fault. You have made poor decisions. You have not been able to hire, retain, and lead a strong leadership team that succeeds. Effective leaders take ownership not only of tasks, but also of the results they generate together with their teams."

After a bit of silence, Felix asked, "What does this have to do with debt? You asked me if I knew the term 'leadership debt'."

"If you buy into the idea that startup failure can always be attributed to bad leadership decisions, founders incur leadership debt every second, minute, hour, and day they postpone working on developing their leadership skills and building a strong leadership team. Every time they postpone working on their transition from founder to leader, they incur leadership debt. The same holds true for managers in big corporations. If they want to climb the career ladder and become leaders, they will eventually have to lead teams. And if these teams fail, it is the manager's fault. He or she has not made the transition from manager to leader. They have waited too long to work on their leadership skills and personal transformation. They have incurred too much leadership debt."

"Like the leadership drama triangle, this is an interesting concept, I must confess. Although, it may mean my investor is right when he says I'm a bad leader."

"You are not necessarily immediately a *bad* leader. But there might be room for improvement. If I recall correctly, your Chief Revenue Officer said something about bad team dynamics. And your country manager accused you of being a bad listener. These are typical leadership debt symptoms. Bad team dynamics and unconstructive finger pointing and blaming—these are leadership debt symptoms."

"Leadership debt symptoms? Are there more?"

"There are many. I will give you a few examples. Let us start with team conflicts. Team conflict and team members blaming each other is a clear symptom you have incurred leadership debt. As an effective leader, you want constructive team discussions—during which team members share diverse points of view and give critical feedback, including peer and upward feedback to you as the leader. This is essential for team success. But there is a big difference between constructive team discussions and team members playing the blame game. If team members start blaming each other, if they start finger pointing, they become unconstructive. This is unhealthy and requires you as the leader to step in."

Felix nodded. What Sophia was saying made perfect sense.

"Another leadership debt symptom is decision-making stagnation. It usually occurs if leaders want to—or have to—approve too many decisions. While leaders have to retain the decision-making power for the most important decisions, they should delegate the rest to the team. I would say that ninety percent of all decisions should be made by the team. Correspondingly, the leaders must empower their team members to make their own decisions. Otherwise, they become a bottleneck.

Then there's high employee turnover. Strong talent wants to work for strong leaders. If leaders fail to attract and retain the right talent, this may be a sign of something being wrong in the leadership team—which certainly includes the leader. This reminds me a bit of what you told me about your HR situation. Makes sense, Felix?"

"Yes, makes sense. But here's a question: Can I repay leadership debt?" Felix asked. "Let's assume you're right, Sophia, and I've incurred leadership debt. Can I repay it?"

"Great question, Felix. First of all, if we assume you have incurred leadership debt, you must become the owner of your leadership debt and accept that you must improve. In fact, all leaders can improve. The leadership path is never over. All leaders are a work in progress. If you start developing your leadership skills, you can avoid incurring even more leadership debt. But you can do more. You can repay some leadership debt by reversing some of your bad leadership decisions. If I recall correctly, you said it was your investor who wanted you to grow faster and faster and to not care about growth efficiency. Why not correct this decision?"

"Because I won't be the CEO anymore tomorrow."

"Felix," Sophia said, "theoretically, this is a decision you could reverse. You could change the growth strategy and pursue a less aggressive growth strategy, no?"

"Yes, theoretically I could do this." Felix thought for a while about what he'd just heard. Then he asked, "Is there also leadership debt that *cannot* be repaid?"

"Yes, some leadership debt cannot be repaid. And you carry this debt load until the end. Until the exit when you sell your business, or the point in time where you close shop."

"What leadership debt is that?"

"Well, there are some leadership decisions that are almost irreversible. Think about your decision to start your venture together with your co-founder Mark. If this decision to build a business with Mark was wrong and if Mark was a bad co-founder, or if you together were a bad team, it would be almost impossible to remedy this. You cannot just exchange a co-founder who is also a big shareholder. The same holds true for the decision to work with a specific investor. As soon as the investor has invested in your company, you are stuck with that investor. This is great if the investor is a good fit, but it is really, really, really bad if you do not get along well with him or her. There is a famous

American investor named Mark Suster, and he once said, 'There is no divorce clause in investment agreements between founders and investors."

"Yeah—unfortunately!"

"What do you mean?"

"I mean that I should have chosen a different investor. We had several offers on the table. I could have chosen someone else."

"Why did you choose your investor then?"

"Because Peter offered the best terms. It was the highest valuation."

Sophia raised her left eyebrow and asked, "You chose your investor based on the valuation *only*?"

Felix sighed. "Yep."

"What did your co-founder think? And your business angel?"

"They both wanted us to go with a different investor, one that Douglas had introduced to us."

"Your business angel."

"Yes. He knows the investor personally and recommended we accept his terms. He said the valuation was lower, but the person's thinking was more aligned with ours. Douglas thought this guy would also bring a lot of industry knowledge to the table."

"And you made the decision to go with Peter?"

"Yes, I did. In hindsight, it seems this was a poor leadership decision. I've incurred leadership debt, no? Leadership debt I can't repay?"

"Unfortunately, I think so, Felix."

"Okay," Felix said. "Let's assume for a moment that I agree with you and everybody else that it is more or less my fault that we're in this situation and that I want to become a better leader."

"Sure, let's assume this."

"The problem I'm facing and that I've always faced is that there are a lot of books out there talking about leadership. What I've always been missing is a structured leadership guide that provides me with actionable insights and frameworks I can use and apply to develop myself further as a leader. I've never really known where to start."

"I know what you mean, Felix. And to be honest, I faced the same problem a few years ago. As I told you, I am the CEO of a family business. We make billions in revenue. You can definitely say it is a decent and large business. I inherited it from my father who had died too young. When I took over the reins as CEO from my father, I had only worked as a strategy consultant previously for a few years. After having been appointed CEO, I sensed people were talking behind my back—the kind of gossip where managers said I was only at the top because of my family roots and that I was too young to lead. This kind of stuff. But, honestly, I did indeed struggle. I understood strategy, I had a good management education, and I had certainly also attended a few classes about leadership. But I did not have any clue about how to lead this business effectively."

"What did you do?"

"Fortunately, one of my best friends had worked with an executive coach who had helped him become a better leader. My friend introduced me to this coach, whom I have been working with ever since. I have been learning a lot from him. He is the one who told me about the drama triangle. And he also shared with me valuable leadership development frameworks that still help me, day in and day out. But there is one overarching framework that helped me to think about leadership in a very structured way. And this may be the kind of framework that you are missing, too. It is called The Leadership House. Interested in hearing more about it? I am happy to share."

"Yes, absolutely," Felix replied. "What is The Leadership House?"

THE LEADERSHIP HOUSE FOUNDATION

"Earn trust, earn trust, earn trust. Then you can worry about the rest."

—Seth Godin

"Before I start," Sophia said, "it cannot hurt if we press the alarm button again." She pressed it, but... nothing. Again, no alarm. Just silence.

"Shouldn't we try and shout? Maybe someone will hear us," Felix said.

Sophia agreed, and she and Felix began yelling, "Help! Help! Can anyone hear us? Hello? Help!" But, again, nothing.

"Do you think we've got enough air in here?" Felix asked, suddenly sounding a bit concerned. He hadn't thought about the air flow before.

"Yes, of course. This old, broken elevator has more holes than Swiss cheese. There's enough air in here. Are you okay, Felix?"

"Yes, but I'd feel better if you started telling me about The Leadership House. I need some distraction again."

"Sure. The Leadership House." Sophia opened her handbag, which perfectly suited her style. It was fancy, just like her. Felix didn't recognize the brand name on the handbag, but he knew it wasn't the brown Louis Vuitton bag that so many women carried, the one that's so overused that its value as a status symbol has diminished over time. Sophia's bag seemed extraordinary. It was a small black handbag with a slim style made from croc-effect leather and a vintage-inspired hinge clasp. Sophia reached into her handbag and took out her red lipstick. "Since we have been stuck in this elevator for quite some time already, I hope they do not mind me painting a bit." With her lipstick, Sophia drew a horizontal rectangle on one of the elevator walls. The red color was rather subdued, but bright enough that the rectangle stood out against the brown elevator wall. Sophia turned to Felix and asked, "Every house needs a solid foundation, right? What do you think is the solid foundation of The Leadership House? What is the basis of effective leadership?"

Felix thought for a moment. Then he responded, "It's probably the vision the leader has. No vision, no followers, right?"

"The vision is important. I agree. The vision must be strong and ambitious. It must be inspiring so that it attracts strong talent. No inspiring vision, no strong followers. No strong followers, no strong team. And no strong team, no leadership success. All of that is correct. But the vision is not the foundation of The Leadership House. Rather, I would say the vision is your North Star, high up in the sky above your Leadership House." Sophia took her lipstick and drew a big circle above the rectangle and wrote the words 'Inspiring Vision' inside it.

"I've also heard people talking about a company's purpose," Felix said, examining Sophia's elevator artwork. "Are purpose and vision the same?"

"For me, they are not—not quite. But there is also not a clear-cut difference, either. For me, the purpose stands for the *why*. Your purpose answers the question of why your company exists. So—what is the purpose of DGTLY, Felix?"

"To help small- and medium-sized businesses become more digital and, thereby, help them succeed."

"Sounds to me that you have a great purpose. Now, let us turn to the vision. Vision stands for the *what*. It stands for what you or your company want to achieve. The vision can be monetary or non-monetary—it depends on the company. For most companies, the vision can be defined with numbers. For instance, a certain revenue or EBITDA number. What is your vision?"

"My vision has always been to build a business with more than one hundred million in revenue. Is this compelling and inspiring?"

"Not on its own, I would say. I suggest you define your vision always in connection with your company's deeper purpose. Your vision is the following: building a business with a hundred million in revenue that helps small- and medium-sized customers become more digital and succeed. In my view, this is quite a powerful and inspiring vision. Try again, Felix—what could be the foundation of The Leadership House?"

Felix scratched his forehead. "What about the team? You said it was all about the team, didn't you? No team, no success, right?"

"Yes, that is what I said. A strong team is important. And I will get back to this very important pillar of The Leadership House shortly."

Sophia took her lipstick out again and drew a vertical rectangle on the left-hand side of the horizontal one. She wrote the words 'Strong Team' inside this rectangle, looked at Felix, and said, "A strong team is the first pillar of The Leadership House. The foundation of The Leadership House, however, is trust." She then wrote 'Trust' inside the horizontal rectangle. "Trust is the major foundation of The Leadership House and the indispensable prerequisite for effective leadership. If there is no trust in the team, the team will always fall short of its potential." She then placed her lipstick back into her bag.

Felix sighed. "Really? First this villain—victim—rescuer—drama triangle theory. Then leadership debt. And now this intangible buzzword. *Trust.* Really?"

"Well, I agree that the word 'trust' is pretty elusive. But trust is nevertheless indispensable. If you think trust is intangible, why don't we try to get some kind of handle on it? How would you describe your relationship with your investor? Peter was his name, no?"

"Yes. You're really a good listener," he smiled at her. "Peter is his name."

"Would you say that you have a trusting relationship with him?"

"Nope. Have you forgotten that he wants to fire me? I obviously cannot trust him."

"Well, I understand you are frustrated because he wants to remove you from office. But this is a consequence of what happened before, right? How had your relationship been prior to this? Trusting? Or full of mistrust?"

Felix didn't have to think long about this. "I think I've never really trusted Peter," he responded. "During the negotiations of his investment terms, he'd asked for the right to unilaterally remove me from office. Why would you ask for such a right if you're a trustworthy person?"

"Well, did you ask him why he wanted to have this right?"

"Nope. I assumed he had some kind of hidden plan. I just told him, 'no way'."

"I cannot say whether he had a hidden plan or not, Felix. But I can tell you that people tend to tell themselves stories. They see something and conclude that what they see means this or that. Have you ever walked down the street, saw someone you knew, wanted to greet him or her, and then that person turned away from you as if he or she had not seen you?"

"Yes. This has absolutely happened. I mean, I'm not supposed to like everyone and not everyone is supposed to like me."

"See, Felix, this is exactly what I mean. You saw this person behaving in a certain way and concluded that person did not like you. But what if that person had just forgotten his or her eyeglasses or had lost his or her contact lenses? Maybe this person just did not see you. Possible?"

"This is a made-up situation."

"Yes, it is made up. But couldn't there be other reasons why that person behaved the way they did?"

"Sure. It's at least possible."

"Indeed. And the same holds true for your investor's behavior. He *might* have had a hidden plan to remove you from office. But I know that investors also have a fiduciary duty towards their shareholders and are sometimes required to ask for these kinds of rights. These rights give them comfort so that they can act accordingly if something ever goes materially wrong. My point is that there are other possible reasons for his behavior. And the story about the hidden plan? That is just a story you told yourself. So—how can you avoid telling yourself stories?"

"By communicating with the other person, I guess?"

"Correct. By communicating. You can avoid telling yourself stories if you simply communicate, if you ask questions and actively listen to what the other person has to say. By listening to *understand*, not just to simply *reply*. If you want to truly understand someone, if you want to understand the other person's goals, intentions, and drivers, you must communicate with the other person. You must listen to them."

"What does this have to do with trust?"

"Felix, if you want someone to trust you, and if you want to figure out whether you can trust him or her, you must communicate. To build trust, you must build genuine relationships. Do not tell yourself stories. Be empathetic! Be emotionally intelligent!"

"Oh, geez, another buzz-phrase—'emotional intelligence'."

It is a bit of a buzz-phrase, yes. Many people have a vague or a false understanding of what emotional intelligence means. But effective leadership is only possible if the leader is being trusted and trusts his team members, and also if the team members trust each other. This requires everybody to build genuine relationships. And this, in turn, requires them to be emotionally intelligent."

"So then what's the exact definition of being emotionally intelligent?" he asked her, a bit sheepish that he didn't already know the answer.

"Emotional intelligence is not so difficult to define," Sophia explained. "It is the ability to understand the way people feel and react. It includes the ability to use this understanding to make good judgments and to avoid or solve problems. If you want to build relationships—and you *must* build genuine relationships with people that you want to trust and be trusted by—you must focus on what matters for the other person. You must ask questions and actively listen to what they have to say. You must put yourself into their shoes and imagine how they may be feeling. And then you can appropriately act upon what you have learned."

"Okay, okay. I understand that I have to be emotionally intelligent if I want to build genuine relationships. And that I have to build genuine relationships if I want to be trusted, or to trust someone. Understood."

"Felix, I understand that you did not ask Peter about his real intentions and reasons when he requested the right to remove you from office. But have you been able to build a relationship with him anyway? A *genuine* relationship, I mean?"

"No, the relationship was difficult from the very beginning. I wouldn't say we built a real relationship at all. We kept our interactions to a minimum."

"How were your board meetings then? Constructive, unconstructive, full of anger? How were they?"

"I would say they were absolutely useless. I ran the board through the numbers, and that was it. More of a reporting forum."

"But the company performance had been falling short of expectations. Did you not have discussions around the reasons for the underperformance?"

"Peter certainly asked what had been going on and what the root causes were."

"And what did you say?"

"I referred to the macroeconomic situation and the high turnover in the leadership team." Felix paused for a moment. "But to be honest, I must confess: I didn't give him the whole picture." Slightly embarrassed, he continued, "I noticed pretty quickly after our last financing round that we wouldn't achieve our plan. The plan showed nice growth, the kind of growth that investors want to see. But we couldn't live up to it."

"Who created the plan?"

"I created the plan together with Mark, and also Nick, our CFO. We knew that investors wanted to see us double our revenues year over year. So, we created such a plan and made some assumptions around the expenses we would incur to achieve it."

"And what about the rest of the leadership team? Marketing, sales, product, tech?"

"We didn't include them. We had to come up with this high-growth plan anyway if we wanted to find an investor. So there was no sense in including anybody else."

"And what happened?"

"We got the money."

"Yes, you got the money. But if I understand you correctly, you have not been able to achieve the plan?"

"Yep. That's our problem. We've been missing our targets month over month."

"What did your team members say?" she asked him. "I mean, I know what your Chief Revenue Officer said and what your UK country manager said. But what about the rest?"

"Not much. It was more that I had to ask them to level up. But they didn't, and they started blaming each other. Marketing blamed sales for not closing enough deals, and sales blamed marketing for not having generated good leads that our salespeople could convert into customers. And our sales guys also blamed product for not having provided the product features many customers asked for. Then our product guys, finger pointed towards our techies for not developing the expected product features fast enough. And..." Felix sighed. "And our techies stressed they first had to work on the stability of our tech infrastructure before they could work on product features. A complete mess."

"Reminds me a bit of a leadership debt symptom, no?"

"Yeah, sounds like it."

"If I hear this correctly, Felix, I honestly wonder how you got so far. Do not get me wrong, but given what I have heard to this point, I am at least a bit surprised that Peter invested twenty million in your company."

"Well, up until Peter's investment, the team had functioned well. It all started after the financing round."

"Why, exactly?" she pressed him. "Do you know?"

"Until we came up with the new plan, we'd been very focused on growing quickly in Germany. And we'd focused on small- and medium-sized business customers only. We'd known what these customers expected in terms of product features.

We'd been good at generating leads to these potential customers. And our sales force had converted those leads nicely into customers, every month. We'd been running like a well-oiled machine, which is also why Peter wanted to invest in us. We'd been really good. But in order to grow faster, we had to expand internationally. We had to develop new products and product features, and we decided to also sell to enterprise clients."

"A lot of complexity."

"Yes, I agree. It got really complex. And it felt as if we're building the rocket while flying."

"I understand," Sophia said. "I have seen these kinds of problems before. Complexity is a growth killer. When did you inform your shareholders about the complexity and the problems you had been facing?"

"In our last board meeting. Peter said during that meeting, 'Felix, if you are not telling me what's going on, I'll retain advisory firms to look into all issues.'"

"And then you told him everything."

"Not necessarily everything, but a lot."

"And what did Peter say when you told him about the mess?"

"He was beside himself with rage. He shouted at me. He said he'd lost his patience with me. He said he knew he couldn't trust me and that I should have told him earlier."

"Not really a surprise, I must say. But there is also a lesson to be learned here, Felix. Do you know what lesson?"

"That trust has been an issue?"

"Yes. Trust has been an issue. Trust is so important because, in a trusting environment, people do not fear to speak up. They disclose problems early on. The beauty of trust and transparency is that it enables a team to work jointly on problem solving. The team can tap into the knowledge and experience of all team members. In your example, I am sure Peter has invested in many companies and sits on many startup boards. He has seen similar problems before. And if you had told him early on what was happening, he might have worked with you and your teams on solving your problems. The same holds true for Douglas. As a business angel, he looks at hundreds of companies each year. Douglas might have helped you, too. Not to mention your leadership team. If you had included them in the planning process—provided you had created a trusting environment—they would have told you what will work and what will not. Together, you might have come up with a plan with less complexity yet still decent growth. For instance, you could have focused on growing faster in Germany only by also selling to enterprise customers. Or you could have continued to focus on small- and medium-sized business customers in some attractive expansion markets. There are always options."

"I get your point, Sophia," Felix said, thoughtfully.

"Felix, you may find trust intangible. But trust and mistrust can make or break your plans to create a massively valuable business. If you have mistrust in the top leadership team and mistrust in the board, you have a dysfunctional team. A dysfunctional team will inevitably entail a dysfunctional organization. And a dysfunctional organization will never succeed. In contrast, if team members trust each other, they call out bad behavior, they challenge one another, they give input, and they help each other. If trust is present, it is always about the issue, *not* the person. Trust should be present among peers and between the leader and the team. Trust is powerful and a competitive advantage. A culture of trust can move mountains."

After a short pause, Sophia continued, "You said that your UK country manager had told you that you would not be able to reach your goals, that the go-to-market strategy would need to be changed. This guy spoke up, did he not?"

"Yep."

"And you fired him. What do you think firing this person showed everyone else in the organization? Did you show that you appreciate people speaking up and challenging you? Did you encourage the rest of your organization to disagree with you? Or have you actually muzzled them?"

"I... muzzled them?" Felix didn't want this to be the correct answer, but he knew that it was true.

"I think so," Sophia said with a sympathetic smile. "It demonstrated that you did not want anyone to question the plan and to speak up. With this kind of behavior, you muzzle your team and kill trust. People get terrified, and terrified teams do not function well. In trusting environments, team members are not terrified. Rather, they feel psychologically safe. And this feeling of safety enables them to say what they think. Creating a feeling of psychological safety is a growth enabler. It extracts the best out of teams and from each team member."

Felix felt discouraged and looked down to the frayed elevator carpeting. Sophia quickly waved her hands in front of his eyes and said, "No, no, no! Felix, do not react that way. There is no reason to look like this. Listen, being a leader is difficult—you know that. There are so many leadership challenges. It is tough. But leadership can be learned. And it starts by realizing that trust is the foundation of effective leadership. Start your leadership journey by embracing trust, by trusting people, and by building relationships built upon trust."

"You make it sound so easy!" Felix replied with a sigh. "How do I build trust, Sophia? I know that being trusted starts by trusting others. But is there more I should know and that could help me start the journey correctly? Any advice here from you?"

"As you know already, I do not really like the word 'advice'. It puts me in the rescuer role and keeps you in the victim role. Not good places to be in. However, my coach has written a leadership guide. In this guide, he shares many leadership development frameworks. And he also shares a framework for building trust. It is called the RESPECT framework."

Sophia took out her lipstick again and wrote 'RESPECT' on the elevator wall, one letter below the other.

"Here. This is what the framework means in a nutshell." Then, beside the vertical letters she'd just written, she made them into full words:

Relationship

Emotional Intelligence

Skills

Professionalism

Empowerment

Consistency

Transparency

"I cannot explain the whole concept here in the elevator," she said as Felix examined the words. "But I will try to summarize all the elements of the RESPECT framework. To build trust, you have to build genuine relationships. We talked about this. You have to be authentic and honest about it. There is no sense in pretending. Your team members would notice. The *R* stands for *relationship.*

"To build genuine relationships, you must be *emotionally intelligent*—this is the *E*. We have covered this, too. Show empathy. Be curious and interested in your team members, both personally and professionally. What are their goals? What do they like and dislike? Go out for a beer with them. If they tell you something, focus on listening to what they have to say. Do not listen simply to just reply. Do not interrupt. Be an active listener who listens to understand.

"The *S* stands for *skills*. If your team members are supposed to trust you and your judgments, you must possess a good skill set. You do not have to know more than your team members in their area of expertise. In fact, you should hire people who are better than you. But you must also be knowledgeable enough to ask the right questions and give guidance. And, most importantly, these skills include your leadership skills.

"Always act *professionally*—this is the *P*. A no-brainer, you may think, but it is still worth mentioning. If you do not act professionally, people will start mistrusting you. Believe me, as a leader, you are a role model. Your teams will watch you 24/7, or at least when you are around. If you act unprofessionally or unethically—even just once—they will expect you to do so again. Mistrust will creep in."

"Okay," Felix said, taking mental notes of everything Sophia was saying. This stuff was good. Really good.

"The other *E* stands for *empowerment*. If you want your team members to trust you, you should trust them, too. But also give them the tools they need to achieve their goals. Empower them to make their own decisions, and then get out of their way. If you have hired the right people, you are not needed. You must not micromanage. Be there for the few—maybe ten percent—of the major decisions you cannot delegate. And then delegate the rest."

"*Empowerment*. Another—"

"I know what you are going to say. Another buzzword. If we have enough time in here, I will get back to *empowerment* in a bit, though."

"And what about the *C*?" Felix asked.

"*Consistency*," Sophia answered, admiring his eagerness. "Be consistent. Walk the talk. Keep your promises. If you do not act consistently, how can your team members trust you?"

Felix nodded.

"And the *T* in *RESPECT* stands for *transparency*. We have already talked about how important transparency is. It is key if you want to build trusting relationships and tap into the knowledge and experience of your team members. Makes sense?" Sophia asked with a smile.

"Makes sense. A lot to be digested. I guess I should read the leadership guide you mentioned as soon as I can... if I can find the time."

"Felix?" Sophia said with a scolding tone.

"Just kidding," he winked. "I know. No more leadership debt. I'll read it."

"Good. What do you think? Ready for the first pillar of The Leadership House?"

"Sure—nothing else to do right now, right?" Felix said with a smile, hoping Sophia could detect his joke. He was actually incredibly interested in the conversation and in what Sophia had to say.

"Then let us continue," she said. "Nobody will change the world alone. Nobody can generate major change by themselves. Irrespective of whether you are a CEO, a founder, a senior manager, or have just been promoted into a leadership position, success will always depend on others. Therefore, the first pillar of The Leadership House is—"

"—a strong team," Felix interjected, completing Sophia's sentence while pointing to the vertical rectangle she had drawn. "But I don't think we need to spend much time on this one. Hire great people, put them into the right positions, and off you go. Simple."

"Well, there *is* a lot of truth to that. If you want to build a highly successful team, you have to hire great talent and put them into the right positions. However, the most important aspect of a strong team would still be missing. But let us approach this in a bit more structured manner."

WHAT MAKES A STRONG TEAM

"The way a team plays as a whole determines its success. You may have the greatest bunch of individual stars in the world, but if they don't play together, the club won't be worth a dime."

—Babe Ruth

B y this point, over an hour had passed since Sophia and Felix first became trapped in the ancient elevator with its faulty alarm system. But they were enjoying talking shop so much that they were beginning to lose track of time, and neither of them minded. Felix was especially enthusiastic; he was soaking up all of Sophia's leadership knowledge, and she was just as eager to share it with him.

"As you said, Felix, to build a strong team, you must hire strong talent and give them the right roles. At least, this is the starting point. Tell me about your team!"

"Okay. Let's start with Mark. Mark is not only my co-founder but also our Chief Operating Officer. We went to university together. Like me, he studied business administration and was awarded a Master of Business Administration degree. We both focused on entrepreneurship and took exactly the same courses. As the two of us worked as bartenders in the evenings, we became aware of how burdensome cash-forecasting was for bar and restaurant managers. And we also realized that scheduling was difficult and took the managers more time than it should. During a business model generation workshop we attended at university, we came up with the business idea of building software that would solve these problems. And that's where everything started."

"I like that," Sophia said, eyebrows raised. "I like founders who understand the industry, see a major problem, and create a solution that solves that problem. I call this *founder/market fit*. Would you consider Mark a strong talent?"

"Yes, absolutely. He was on the Dean's list and finished his studies with distinction. He was better than me."

"Was?" Sophia asked. "He *was* better?"

"Yes, was. I mean he's still very good. But writing a business plan is different from leading a real business. We both agree it's been a good thing that I've become the CEO and he the second-in-command."

"The second-in-command?"

"Yes, Mark covers my back when I am not around. We rarely disagree. And we often know what the other is about to say even before the other says it."

"You rarely disagree," Sophia repeated.

"Yes, it's really great. We're like brothers in spirit."

"Like brothers in spirit."

"Yes. Brothers in spirit, or partners in crime. We just complement each other, you know? Whenever I'm not around, I know I can trust that Mark will represent me appropriately. I don't have to brief him much. He just knows what I'd do and say if I was there."

"You complement each other."

"What are you getting at, Sophia? Are you going to repeat everything I'm saying?" Felix laughed a little, but he wondered what the point of this was. "So yes, we trust each other and want to make this company a huge success. He's my wingman."

"It is good that you trust each other. And it is always good to have a wingman. But I do not yet understand why you think you complement each other. You have not yet told me anything about complementary hard or soft skills. And you rarely disagree. How does this make him a complementary partner, a 'partner in crime', as you said?"

"I can talk with him about my ideas. And he's a good sounding board. He's a good friend, too."

"Felix, how can someone be a good sounding board if that person rarely disagrees with you?"

"Well... he helps me structure my thoughts. He helps me refine my ideas. You name it. He helps in several ways."

"I understand. But let us pause here for a moment. I am on a few startup boards myself, and when I discuss with my fellow board members what to look for in C-Levels, we usually agree that we must look for strong talent with enough gravitas to challenge the CEO. For someone who comes up with different viewpoints and is at ease with disagreeing constructively. It is constructive discussions and disagreements—not constant affirmation—that add value. Put differently: What makes Mark the right person in the right role? What makes him the right Chief Operating Officer for DGTLY?"

"If I'm not mistaken, there's no clear role description for a Chief Operating Officer. There are many different roles Chief Operating Officers can assume in a company. Sometimes, they are the second-in-command, like Mark. Other times, they really focus on operations. The actual responsibilities vary greatly from company to company."

"I agree. The roles that COOs take on vary greatly. For me, but this is only my personal view, the COO must ensure that vision is being translated into reality. And this entails a lot, and it especially requires that person to have great constructive discussions with all leadership team members and to challenge the CEO again and again. I am not saying he has to constantly disagree, but he should challenge the CEO in a constructive manner. Are there other roles Mark could assume?"

"Sure. As I said, he is very talented. We've already discussed whether he'd better suit a Chief Strategy Officer role, for instance."

"Hmmm. Well, at the end of the day, you must assess whether Mark is the right person in the right role. But let me share a story with you. I have been on the board of directors of a Dutch high-growth tech company. In a board meeting once, our CEO told the board that his co-founder would step down from the Chief Marketing Officer position. He was supposed to become the Chief Strategy Officer. When we asked the CEO why his co-founder stepped down, he told us that the co-founder reflected on his strengths and weaknesses and concluded he was not the right person to lead the marketing department anymore. He thought the company had outgrown his skills. He thought he was good at generating initial traction. He thought he was a decent marketing expert, but he did not feel comfortable leading a big marketing organization. This guy was very self-aware. And I admired him for his selfless decision to step down. But when we asked the CEO why his co-founder had been the right person for the Chief Strategy Officer role, he could not give us a good answer. He stammered and said, 'He could also be a good Chief Partnership Officer.' To all the board members, it became clear that the CEO was just looking for a role his co-founder and friend could assume in order to remain with the company. But this is not 'having the right people in the right seats', as they say. In fact, if you start giving people jobs not because they are the best for the job, but because you have a personal relationship with them, you are already off track. You not only lack the best talent, you also demotivate the rest of the team."

"Why?"

"Because you show your team that you do not hire for and expect high performance. You show them that you are fine with mediocrity."

"Mark is not mediocre," Felix assured her.

"I have not said so, Felix. I am not judging. It is your job to build a high-functioning team. It is your job to assess whether Mark is the right person in the right role. It is just that sometimes certain people are the right person in the right role for a specific period of time only. Sometimes, if the company or the tasks have outgrown the skills and passions of that person, it is time for the person to move on."

"I understand, Sophia. That makes a lot of sense. I guess I have to think about this."

"That's fine. Think about it. And have an open discussion with Mark about this. It should not be a problem, as you really seem to have a trusting relationship. Who else is in your leadership team?"

"There's our CFO, Nick. He has a Master of Finance degree. He joined three years ago immediately after his graduation and after Peter had invested in our company. He took over finance from me so I could focus more on other leadership stuff. He's our Excel mastermind. You won't find a single bug in our financial models. Believe me, he's doing an awesome job. We call him 'No Hiccups Nick'."

"He keeps your house in order?"

"Yes. All good in our finance department. Our marketing department—"

"Wait, Felix. Did you not say earlier that you are not achieving your plans?"

"Yes, this is unfortunately true, but that's not Nick's fault. As I said, the product isn't yet satisfying the needs of our customers in our expansion markets and of our enterprise clients. There's still a lot to do in product, tech, and marketing."

"And all this is not something that 'No Hiccups Nick' should have taken into account when building the budget and the financial model?" Sophia asked.

"He wanted to, but then our plan would have been less attractive, you know? As I said, VCs and business angels want to see bullish plans that show impressive growth. Otherwise, they don't invest. I therefore insisted we create an ambitious plan that we could achieve if all the pieces fell into the right places. For this, we unfortunately had to create the complexity we talked about earlier." Felix paused before adding, "Or maybe not. But it's too late now."

"And Nick came up with this wonderful plan. Without further discussion, right? And without further liaising with and including the rest of the team?"

"Yes. These are the judgment calls I must make as a leader, no? I wanted to see an ambitious plan and ambitious goals so my teams could strive for achieving them. The team would have questioned all this. And we might have failed to raise the money. But maybe you are right—maybe I should have included the team in the planning process. Isn't that what you're getting at?"

"Felix. I also invest in startups and if there is one thing I hate, it is unrealistic growth plans. They lead to chaos and mistrust. If teams are not included in establishing the plan or do not deem the plan realistic for other reasons, then they do not care about the plan at all. They just continue working as they had been doing before. This has nothing to do with smart business steering. And what about the investors?"

"What about the investors? It's their decision to invest."

"They invest in your company on the basis of a plan only to hear in the first board meeting that you are going to *miss the plan.* And you are going to miss the plan again and again. How can your investors trust you if they realize shortly after their investment that you either deceived them or cannot steer your business properly. Or, even worse, if you deceived them *and* cannot steer the business?"

"Everybody does this, Sophia. This is the startup world."

"No. Sorry, but this is not true" she shook her head. "As a business angel, I indeed meet many founders who are like this, but I give them a wide berth. I focus on the ones who are smart and honest, founders with whom I can build trusting relationships. I prefer startups with realistic growth plans. And I prefer CFOs who can drive growth successfully. Plans are only plans, but a CFO should be able to establish a plan that the teams do not miss constantly. Could 'No Hiccups Nick' have come up with this kind of plan, Felix?"

"Yeah, I guess so."

"Then he is a still junior, but strong talent in the right position?"

"Yes, I think so."

"Okay then. Let us move on. Who is next?"

"Next, we've got Mick, our VP of Marketing, and Steve, our VP of Sales and Customer Success. As I said before, they'd been working well together as a team until we gave them the new plan. Mick had been generating enough leads to potential customers and Steve's sales team converted them nicely into paying customers. What I really liked about them was their strong cooperation. If problems came up, they stuck their heads together and solved them amicably. This dynamic totally changed after I presented them the new plan."

"Was it anything they said with regard to the new plan?"

"No, although I could definitely sense their disbelief in it. Still, I encouraged them. I said, 'Guys, I know this is an ambitious plan. But let's go for it and nail it.' But they wouldn't pull it off. So we hired our Chief Revenue Officer. We hired Ralf and decided Steve and Mick, who had reported to me, would report to Ralf as his VP of Marketing and VP of Sales and Customer Success."

"And how did they like this move?"

"Not at all. I mean, I can understand that. They'd been C-Levels and became VPs. But these are only titles. And that's also what I told them. I told them that this was only a reorganization and that I still needed them to perform as always. But since then, Mick's and Steve's work attitude has become unacceptable."

"What was on your mind when you hired Ralf?"

"What do you mean?"

"I mean, why did you hire him in the first place?'"

"To fix our growth issues."

"But did you not say that your growth issues stemmed from your plan and from not having the product ready yet, among other issues you faced?"

"Yep. But Peter requested we hire a Chief Revenue Officer, because he said he'd seen this working in other companies. He said that Chief Revenue Officers could create alignment among marketing, sales, and customer success, and therefore ignite growth."

"And at that point in time, you had not yet shared with the board the actual reasons for your problems, had you?"

"No. That came later."

"See, Felix—this happens if you act in an environment of mistrust," she told him. "If you are not transparent about your problems, how can your team members help you? Think about it: if you had disclosed the actual problems, your investor would have noticed that hiring a Chief Revenue Officer might not be the right solution for your problem. I agree with Peter in the sense that a Chief Revenue Officer is the right hire in situations where marketing, sales, and customer success underperform, fight, are not aligned, and must be guided by one person with overall responsibility. But in your case, where the problem mainly stemmed from product and the complexity arising from expanding internationally, adding new products and product features, and targeting a new customer segment, the Chief Revenue Officer is not the solution to the problem. It is no wonder Ralf left again. He probably realized he could not create value. In addition, he had to work with a demotivated team. If you are surprised that Mick and Steve do not show the right work attitude anymore, try to put yourself into their shoes. What goes on in their minds?"

"I don't know. They have great jobs. And we have a great market opportunity. I don't get it. Being a VP is great, isn't it?"

"How do you think they felt when you hired Ralf and changed the reporting line? Did they feel like being promoted?"

"No, probably not," Felix reflected. "But I told them it wasn't a demotion. It was only a reorganization."

"But it must have felt like a demotion anyway. And it certainly looks like a demotion on their CVs. And on top of those things, you hired someone to solve a problem that was nonexistent. What do you think they thought about this?"

"Well, they told me that it wouldn't make sense to hire a Chief Revenue Officer. But what could I do? That was what the board wanted."

"The board is in charge of supervising and helping you. The board is supposed to create value for you. And sometimes they have the right to say no to what the management team wants to do. But they are not in charge of building your team. They should *help* you build the team. They should interview potential hires. They should have discussions with the members of the leadership team. But no, Felix, it is *you* who are in charge of building a strong leadership team. Anyway, so Ralf has left the company. What now?"

"I wanted to replace him. But what you've just said makes me think this might not be a good decision. If we assume that a Chief Revenue Officer doesn't actually solve our problem, I don't have to replace him. Also, maybe Mick's and Steve's work attitudes will change again if I shift everything back to what the organization structure looked like before."

"Felix, to me, this sounds like a reasonable discussion you should have with your team."

"Ah, absolutely. I will discuss this with the team and the board."

Sophia laughed. "Exactly."

"Then we have our Chief Technology Officer," Felix continued. "All's fine with Tim and our tech team, I would say. Tim is a nerd. You know, a real techie. Started coding already during high school and had worked for some of the big US companies before he returned to Germany. He's one of these magical hires. This guy could have worked anywhere, but he decided to join our rocket ship. And he delivered on what he had promised. He's in his late forties already. I sometimes wish he wouldn't push back so hard on product feature development. But he says that we'll 'inevitably fail if we don't ensure our technology is stable, secure, and scalable.' He always says that 'product development and tech infrastructure work must be in balance.' And I trust his judgment. And honestly, I don't know better anyway. On top of that, Pete, our Chief Product Officer, agrees with this assessment. I'm absolutely fine with both Tim and Pete."

"Sounds good. Are they German?"

"Yes."

"And all the others as well? Former Chief Revenue Officer, CFO, VP of Sales, VP of Marketing, Chief Operating Officer, and yourself? And all white?"

"Yes. One could say we're probably not the most diverse team on earth."

Sophia laughed heartily. "Well, this is a nice one, Felix. You are a bunch of white German males. You may have different academic backgrounds—and that is not even true for you and Mark. But that is it. No diversity at all, Felix."

"Listen, we hire the best," he told her, a little irritated. "And if the best talent is male, we hire a male. I don't like all this 'women's quota' stuff. I don't want to discriminate anyone, whether they're male or female."

"Well, I am not saying that you should discriminate anyone. I am, however, a bit surprised that you could not find any female, any non-German, any non-white professional who was at least as good as your current team members. At the very least, I have a hard time believing this. But we are slowly getting to the core of what it takes to build a strong team. How do you create a strong team? What do you think?"

"Well, we've established that I must hire great talent and put them in the right roles. But obviously, I'm missing something."

"Yes, you are. Your job as a leader is not to hire the best people for each discipline. Your job as a leader is not to hire the best finance talent, nor the best marketing talent, and so on. What *is* your job as a leader?"

"To hire the best team?" Felix asked, hoping it was the answer she was looking for.

"That is right, Felix—that is exactly right. You must assemble the best team. Let me go back to your boys' club for a moment. Do you think that it is a good team setup? Or, let me ask this differently. How might a better setup look?"

"I guess a better setup would also have some female team members, right?"

"Right," she agreed. "But it is not only about male and female. Diversity and inclusion have many facets. The main reason why studies confirm that diverse teams outperform non-diverse teams is that diverse teams can look at problems from different perspectives. Diverse teams can come up with a greater variety of options to tackle and overcome challenges. If you want to hire for diversity, you look for people who are different from you, who have complementary skills, who come from different geographies. The list goes on. Eventually, it is all about the team. You not only want to hire the best talent, but also assemble a set of individuals whose backgrounds add to the group. You can sense it. You hire people who are strong individuals and who jointly represent a strong team. And in the leadership team, you also hire for leadership skills, right? Otherwise, you would try to build a leadership team, but in fact build a management team. Managers are important, yes. But you need leaders around you to be successful in the long run."

"Okay. I understand. It's all about the team. It's all about assembling a strong set of individuals with leaderships skills. Individuals who act as a team. Can I ask you a question, Sophia?"

"Sure. Go ahead."

"Assembling a strong team probably includes firing people when I sense that they're not a good fit, right?"

"Of course. To fire someone is probably one of the toughest decisions leaders have to make, but it is part of the leader's job. What is on your mind?"

"Well, we have a senior developer in the team who constantly disagrees with our decisions. If we decide to buy a specific software, she believes we should build it on our own. If we decide to prioritize developing a specific product feature that helps us get closer to product/market fit, she wants to focus on another feature. I mean, I understand that it's good that people disagree, but this lady makes me go crazy. And she just does what she wants."

"Anything else?"

"Yes, she's been with us since almost the beginning. She was one of the first developers we hired. Everybody likes her. And she's influential. I don't want to fire her. The team will hate me for it."

"Is she generally performing well?"

"Not really. And she doesn't get along well with our CTO, either."

"So why do you think people will hate you for firing her? Have you considered that they might hate you for *not* firing her?"

"Why might that be?"

"If your company is anything like companies I have worked for before, your employees have joined your team to win. They have dreams and want to be part of something special. They want to be part of a 'rocket ship', as you put it. And they want this rocket ship to lift up and orbit your North Star. If someone in the team is constantly underperforming without any consequences, other team members may think underperformance is accepted in your company. This normally ignites a death spiral of sorts, in which the best people leave or underperform. And this, in turn, leads to even more underperformance. As a leader, you cannot accept this."

"You think I should fire her?"

"I think that you should deal professionally with her. Talk to her. Try to understand why she is acting the way she is."

"Empathy and emotional intelligence, no?"

"Right. Make it clear that you cannot accept her behavior, but that you are willing to help her. And be honest about your intention to help. You have hired her. You are in charge of the people in your organization. You must ensure they perform. If you have genuinely tried to help her and she has not changed her attitude, you may have to fire her, yes. But if you ultimately do, do so with respect and in a professional manner."

"Thanks, Sophia. This helps. And I think I've understood how to build a strong team. I must hire strong talent with leadership skills. Talent that complements each other and works as a team. Diverse talent that can look at our problems from various perspectives. And I need to let go of people who are not a good fit. And put everybody in the right roles. And ensure they all work as a team. Is this correct?"

"Yes. This is correct. It is not only about hiring strong talent and putting them into the right positions, but also about assembling a diverse team that embraces teamwork. It is teamwork that translates a set of strong individuals into a strong team."

"Understood."

"But I have one more question for you, Felix. It is a question many founders ask me. They say something like, 'This is all good and it sounds great on paper, Sophia. But how do I ensure my strong set of individuals works as a team? How do I create teamwork?' Do you know the answer?"

After a brief pause, Felix replied, "By talking with them about the benefits of working as a team. Communication. Going with them through research reports. Trying to show how teamwork makes a difference in sports. Like Michael Jordan, who said, 'Talent wins games, but teamwork and intelligence win championships.'"

"Good ideas, Felix. Very good. But there are also specific and concrete steps you can take to transform a set of individuals into a strong team. And, essentially, many of The Leadership House pillars that we have not yet talked about help you ensure your team members work as a team. They help you ensure proper teamwork. Interested in the next pillar of The Leadership House?"

"Yes, of course. What pillar comes next?"

CHAPTER 7

SHARING IS CARING

"Our success is directly related to our clarity and honesty about who we are, who we're not, where we want to go, and how we're going to get there."

—Howard Behar

F elix was certainly enjoying these exchanges with Sophia. Yes, she constantly challenged him. But in addition to the conversation helping him forget about his claustrophobia, he was also learning some very interesting things about leadership, things he'd never considered previously. He smiled, realizing he was probably learning more in that elevator than from listening to what the famous guy on the fifth floor was talking about.

"Why are you smiling?"

"Just about how much I'm enjoying this. Who needs the guy upstairs, anyway? Your advice is wonderful. I should have met you earlier. Maybe my situation would look differently than it does currently."

"That is nice of you." She smiled. "It is great to hear that I am helpful. My coach gave me a lot of knowledge, and I am always happy to pass on what I have learned from him. But I doubt I know more than this guy talking upstairs, whoever he is."

Sophia turned to the back wall of the elevator and drew another rectangle. Pointing her forefinger to the *Inspiring Vision* circle drawn above The Leadership House, she said, "Remind me. What was your vision again?"

"To build a business with a hundred million in revenue, one that helps small- and medium-sized businesses become more digital and succeed."

"Sure. If you went out with this great vision and hired a strong team, could you just show your team your North Star and ask them to turn your vision into reality?"

"I guess the fact that you're asking this question means that the answer is no. As we're talking about how to create teamwork, and since our ambitious— and somewhat obviously unrealistic—plan seems to create some problems, I might have to give them a more realistic one, one they can follow. With a realistic plan, the team will work together as a team again. Is this what the next pillar stands for? 'Realistic Plan'?"

"You are on the right track, but no. 'Realistic Plan' is not what we will be writing inside the rectangle. Before you can come up with a realistic plan, what should you be talking about with your team?"

"Ah, yes—talking with the team. I remember this, of course."

Sophia smiled.

Felix thought aloud, "Maybe in more general terms, about how we can pull it off? About how we can turn our vision into reality? So, from a higher-level perspective?"

"Good! You are headed into the right direction. And what is it exactly that you want to talk about? Can you be a bit more precise?"

"I want to talk about what everybody needs to do so that we—as a team—can achieve our vision?"

"Very good. Indeed, very good. When I work with leadership teams, I call this process 'reverse engineering'. In your example, the question that you need to answer and the topic that you want to discuss with your team is what you must do now and in the near future so you can achieve your vision down the line. With your team, you reverse-engineer your vision of building a business with a hundred million in revenue that helps small- and medium-sized business customers become more digital and succeed. You divide this overall vision into smaller goals. After having reverse-engineered your vision into goals, you know the three to five goals you need to achieve now and in the near future to achieve your vision down the line."

"But that's what Mark and I did together with our CFO, no? We set ourselves the goal to achieve a hundred million in revenue and created a plan laying out what we must do in the next years to get there. Where are the revenues supposed to be coming from? From which markets and from which customer segments do we need to generate how much revenue? That's exactly what we did."

"I know. But what was the problem? Why haven't you achieved the plan? Why have you fallen short of it month over month?"

"Because the goals haven't been achievable?"

"Correct," she nodded, smiling in agreement. "You have created goals in terms of revenue you must generate in each of your expansion markets and in each customer segment. And you have probably also created ambitious goals related to the new products you have been developing. But the goals have been unrealistic. Why have they been unrealistic, Felix?"

"Because they've been too ambitious... I mean, the revenue targets have been too high."

"Why have they been too high?"

"Ah, I think I understand what you mean. They've been too high because I set the goals together with Mark and our CFO. We set them without asking our teams for feedback as to whether we could actually achieve the goals?"

"Almost one hundred percent spot on."

"Almost?"

"Bear with me, Felix. I would just phrase it a bit differently. I would not say you have been missing your plan because you did not ask your team for feedback. I would say it is because you did not include the team in the goal-setting process. You did not run the goal-setting process together *with* the team. As you did not run the process *with* the team, but rather *imposed goals* on the team, the team did not buy into the goals. And the team did not buy into the whole plan, either."

"Okay."

"Felix, if you had included the team, what do you think they might have suggested in terms of goals? Let us take just one goal as an example. It is hypothetical, as you did not ask them. But what do you think they might have come up with?"

"Hmmm. One major goal would probably have been that we first generate product/market fit in the expansion markets and the new customer segment. And only after this, we would start investing heavily in selling our products in those markets and customer segment. Yes, that's probably what they would have suggested. But then, we wouldn't have raised the money or wouldn't grow as Peter wants us to grow. Difficult."

"Yes, sometimes life is difficult, especially as a leader. But you are not growing as Peter wants you to grow anyhow. Let us talk about this product/market fit topic in theory a bit further. Regarding the discussion in the team about whether to focus on generating product/market fit, what might the process have looked like?"

"They would have realized they'd not generated product/market fit in some expansion markets and the enterprise client customer segment. They would have concluded they need to solve this. The product team would have sought input from customers, the marketing team, the sales team, and the customer success team about what customers expect and what must be developed. And the product team would have talked with the tech team about the development process and about how the respective product features find their way into the development road map."

"And what about the finance team?"

"They're numbers guys. How could they have helped?"

"Yes, good question. How could they have helped?"

"I don't know," he sighed. Then his eyes lit up and he said, "Okay, they could have calculated the product development costs together with the product and tech teams. Ahh... and they could have calculated how much we could earn selling the products or product features and how this would impact our customer lifetime value."

"Correct. They could have helped you understand whether the costs developing and selling the products make sense given the money you will earn selling the products. They could have helped you assess how the development costs would impact your cash flow and the amount of money you have to raise from investors. They could potentially also have helped you analyze the size of the market for the product or new target customer segment. Right?"

"Yep."

"Then would it not be possible that the goal-setting process—due to the involvement of the finance team—would have ended with a decision not to generate product/market fit in the enterprise customer segment because the economics do not add up?"

"Yes, this might have been the outcome."

"See? There is a lot of input you can get from finance. It is worth including the team, too."

"Hmm. You're right. I get it. Generating product/market fit requires input from all departments."

"Correct. Generating product/market fit is not something that the product team can achieve on its own. You generate product/market fit if you develop products that solve the customer's problem. But solving the customer's problem must be economically meaningful. You are a CEO with a business to lead. The numbers must make sense. And to answer the question about what the required features are, you want input from all departments. All departments must have a seat at the table in some shape or form."

"Okay. So do we write 'Team Goals' inside the rectangle?"

"Almost right. But let me quickly recap. You created your own goals and gave them to your team. As your team had not been involved in the goal-setting process, these goals did not become *their* goals. Your team has not bought into the goals and therefore not into the plan, either. What you should have done instead..." Sophia turned to the elevator wall and wrote 'Shared Goals' inside the rectangle, "... is to create *shared* goals. It is *shared* goals that create team buy-in and teamwork. I must confess, one could also call them 'team goals', but in

The Leadership House framework they are called 'shared goals', so let us stick with that. The point is that you *ask* the team and *discuss* with the team what goals must be achieved in order to turn your vision into reality. The team should come up with the shared goals, not you. This makes them *shared* goals."

"Okay. Understood."

"Felix, why is it actually so powerful to include the team in the goal-setting process? What do you think?"

"Because including them gives the team a feeling of ownership. This feeling of ownership creates buy-in."

"It is not only a *feeling* of ownership, Felix. If the team participates in the goal creation process, if the team comes up with the shared goals, the team *becomes* the owner of the goals. If *they* suggest the goals to work on, the team members become the owners of these goals. They will do whatever they can to achieve them. This ownership aspect is pretty powerful."

"But I guide the goal-setting process, no?"

"Yes, you must be involved. The goal-setting process is very important. Ever heard of the midwife technique? The one that Socrates applied?"

"Socrates? Now you're kidding me, right?"

"Not at all, Felix. Socrates is known for having said, 'He was knowing nothing.' Socrates was not making others wise by sharing his wisdom—rather, he helped others come up with their own ideas. Like a midwife who helps a woman give birth, he helped others become wiser from within. In a nutshell, it is about using questions and giving guidance to help others—in your case, your team—to come up with great ideas—in your case, the shared goals. You can apply this technique in the goal-setting process."

"Wow. That's pretty cool. And who decides at the end of the process which shared goals to pursue?"

"That is a good question. And, in fact, it is a question I have been asked many times before by the leaders I have been working with. The answer is *you*. The ultimate decision-making authority is still you. It is rarely the case that everybody immediately and unanimously agrees with the shared goals your team comes up with. You may encounter different opinions and opposing views, and this is good. This is the dynamic you want to create in your team. But if your team members cannot agree, you must make the ultimate judgment call."

"But are the goals then still their goals? I mean really *shared* goals?"

"Yes. The psychological aspect of ownership in the shared goals does not vanish if the goals have not been agreed upon unanimously. Psychologically, it is important that team members are involved in the shared goal-setting process. They want to be and *must* be heard. Even if they cannot ultimately agree, the goals remain *shared* goals. If done correctly, you create a 'disagree but commit' feeling in the team members who would have decided differently. Long story short: it is still you who calls the shots, but it is not you alone who comes up with the shared goals. It is a joint process in which you as the leader help your team come up with the right goals and where you may have to make final judgment calls."

"Sounds a bit as if I would be tricking my team," he said thoughtfully. "You know, it feels as if I had the answer and just wanted them to come up with the answer... like, I don't want to be the rescuer, if you know what I mean."

"Good that you mention this. Let me stress: like with the relationships you build, the goal-setting process must be genuine. You do not want to have the answer before the process starts. And if you hired better people, people who are better than you, they will hopefully have better answers than you. You run this process to tap into the knowledge and experience of your team members. They should be telling you what to do."

"Doesn't this also require a strong culture? I mean, you want everybody to trust each other, to contribute to the team efforts and processes, and to embrace a 'disagree but commit' attitude. I mean, if you ask me, this is a lot. How many companies are out there that have such a culture?" Felix asked, requiring a bit more light to be shed upon this concept.

"I can tell you that I have worked with founders who managed to build this kind of culture in their teams. But there were certainly also founders who built toxic cultures," Sophia explained. "I have analyzed teams with a great culture and also teams with a toxic culture. I wanted to find out whether I could see patterns. And indeed, I could. These patterns relate to a topic we have already discussed: leadership debt. The ones with toxic cultures incurred too much of it. And that leadership debt stemmed from a leader's poor leadership decision to postpone generating a strong company culture early on. They focused all their efforts *outside* the company. They focused on the market, competition, customers—you name it. But they decided not to work on the *inside*. They did not take care of building a strong culture early on. And—"

"The ones with strong company cultures worked early in the game on building a strong culture. Right?"

"Yes," she affirmed. "They invested in their leadership skills early on. And they did not only include their teams in the goal-setting process. They also included them in the process of defining shared values."

"Shared values?"

"Yes. An inspiring vision, trust, a strong team, and shared goals only bring you so far if your team members do not care at all about *how* they work together. If they are indifferent about the *how,* in terms of how they want to work as a team, the result can be a culture in which personal aspirations and achievements are at the forefront of individual behavior. Teamwork dies. The *how* is equally important as the *why* and the *what.* Strong values are of utmost importance for teamwork and team success. But not only strong values, but *shared* values. Your team members must share strong values."

"'Shared values'. Is this another pillar of The Leadership House framework?"

"Indeed it is. Here—please take my lipstick and write it inside a pillar next to the one called 'Shared Goals'."

Felix took the lipstick and wrote 'Shared Values' inside a vertical rectangle. Afterwards, he gave back the lipstick and asked her, "It's *shared* values because I include the team in the process. Like I do with *shared* goals. Right?"

"Yes, the process is exactly the same. And you should go through this process as early as possible. The first employees of a startup and the first team members of any team set the culture for who and what comes after. Shared values reflect the norms and standards guiding your team members' behaviors. And shared values are the glue that binds vision, shared goals, and, ultimately, performance. You must agree on them as early as possible."

"You mean shared values lead to better performance?" he asked.

"Yes. The link between shared values and performance might not be immediately obvious. But many studies have evidenced the enormous business impact shared values and a strong culture can have. They have confirmed that there is a strong link between high performance and a strong company culture. Felix, I recommend you do not start this process late. But better late than never." Sophia ended her last sentence with a wink.

The elevator lights flickered again.

"The flickering probably means we can move on to the next pillar," Felix said dryly, looking up at the ceiling.

Sophia smiled. "Yes, let us do that. And this time, I will tell you immediately what the next pillar is. You have already said it yourself anyway when you first mentioned a 'realistic plan'."

THE LEADERSHIP SCALE

"I am like the midwife, in that I cannot myself give birth to wisdom. The common reproach is true, that, though I question others, I can myself bring nothing to light because there is no wisdom in me... Of myself I have no sort of wisdom, nor has any discovery ever been born to me as the child of my soul. Those who frequent my company at first appear, some of them, quite unintelligent, but, as we go further with our discussions, some make progress at a rate that seems surprising to others as well as to themselves, although it is clear that they have never learned anything from me. The many admirable truths which they bring to birth have been discovered by themselves from within."

—Socrates

Sophia took her lipstick and wrote 'Joint Plans' inside a new vertical rectangle next to the 'Shared Values' pillar.

"'Joint Plans'? What's the difference between joint plans and shared goals? Isn't this exactly the same?"

"No, they are not the same, Felix. Joint plans are built on the basis of shared goals. But they are different from one another."

"Are they more detailed and tell us exactly what we must do to achieve our goals?"

"Indeed, joint plans are more granular. But I would not say they show the *what*," Sophia said, using virtual quotation marks, "but rather, the *how*." Joint plans have to do with the *how*. But this time, not in terms of values, but in terms of how your team can achieve the shared goals. It is a layer below the one on shared goals. Your financial model, for instance, should reflect your team's joint plan as to how they want to achieve your shared goals."

"And the pillar is not called 'Plans', but '*Joint* Plans', because I involve the team again, right?"

"Correct. Let me, however, stress that you are less involved at this stage," she clarified. "I love another framework I have learned from my coach. It is called the 'Leadership Scale'. Let me share the concept with you. It has always helped me better decide how much I should be involved."

"The leadership scale? Like, how heavy you are? A leadership gorilla?" Felix smiled.

"No," Sophia laughed. "May I?" She gestured with her lipstick that she wanted Felix to move a bit aside so she could draw something on the other wall of the elevator. Felix made some room and Sophia drew a long vertical line onto the wall. At the top of the line, she wrote 'High Involvement' and at the bottom, she wrote 'Low Involvement'. Next to the line on the left she wrote from the top to the bottom: 'Vision', 'Building a Strong Team', 'Shared Values', 'Shared Goals', 'Joint Plans', and 'Execution'. On the right side of the line, she wrote the numbers one to ten, ten being at the top. She finished her new piece of art on the elevator wall by writing 'The Leadership Scale' right above it.

Sophia explained, "If you want to be an effective leader, you cannot and must not be involved in *all* aspects of your business. You must set the vision—maybe together with your co-founders—and build a strong team. But the more you move from vision to execution, the less you can and should be involved. If you have assembled a great team, created a secure environment determined by trust, and have—together with the team—created shared goals and shared values, you can leave the team with the translation of shared goals into specific actions. The more you go down the leadership scale, the more you let go and consciously give up control."

"I give up control?"

"Yes. And that is where many leaders struggle and fail," she cautioned. "They cannot let go, Felix. They do not feel comfortable losing control. They want to be involved in everything. They want to make all the decisions, and by wanting to be involved in all the decisions they become a decision-making bottleneck. Remember, this was a symptom of leadership debt."

"Yes, I remember. I think being involved in everything may work in small organizations with flat hierarchies. But as soon as you lead a big team or a high-growth organization, it doesn't work anymore."

"That is right. Effective leaders, therefore, build a strong team who can make important decisions themselves."

"But in my experience, not everybody feels comfortable making important decisions. For some people, having to make important decisions feels scary."

"That is true," she agreed. "But if you help your team members to become leaders themselves, they will love it. Being empowered to make important decisions motivates team members. In contrast, always having to ask for approval and being micromanaged is demotivating and discouraging for team members. My advice... oh, *whoops*—I have used the 'A word'. So be it. My advice, if I may, is to always think twice about how much you must be involved. Move up and down the leadership scale. On top of the scale is the *why*, your deeper purpose and vision. This is where your involvement is needed the most. This is where you alone make the decision. The more you move down the scale from the *why* to the *what* to the *how*, the less involved you can and should be. This makes you an effective leader, at least if all other leadership house aspects are also observed."

"So I can concentrate on the most important aspects of the business. I can focus on strategy and leave the execution to the team."

"Careful, Felix. I have worked with leaders who thought they could ponder *only* the overall strategy. I worked with one founder in particular who embraced this mindset. He came up with a thirty-page strategy paper and thought he had hired a team to do the actual work. Very dangerous, Felix. Very dangerous. I have been successful helping leaders overcome this challenge by adding another leadership concept to the mix. It is called the 'Three Leadership Altitudes'."

"Another concept your coach developed?"

"Actually, no. This concept has been developed by INSEAD Professor Ian C. Woodward. I attended one of his executive leadership courses, in which he shared this framework. I will spare you the details, but in essence, this concept explains why some leaders are more effective than others. As an effective leader, you cannot just fly high and see the big picture. Effective leaders fly at *all* levels. They smoothly travel up and down easily. Yes, they can fly high and see the big picture. But they can also get down and become involved in the more strategic and even tactical aspects of their teams and business, and, if need be, can go all the way down and get their hands dirty on the ground. In your example, you cannot reduce your leadership work to working on the big and bold ideas, purpose, and vision. You must also be involved in the generation of shared goals. And you must also be involved in joint plans and concrete implementation of tasks if this is required. That is why it says 'Low Involvement' and not 'No Involvement' at the bottom of the leadership scale. Makes sense?"

"Yes, makes sense. If problems arise in the implementation phase, I need to be there for the team and solve the issue."

"Correct. But with regard to 'I solve the issue', let me refer again to the leadership drama triangle. Be careful if team members approach you and ask you for advice, help, or a solution to their problems. If your teams ask you for advice and you give advice, you become the rescuer and the team members become the victims. Do you remember the only way you can escape the drama triangle trap?"

"By stepping out of it. By not becoming or remaining a victim, a villain, or a rescuer."

"Correct. You are a fast learner," she winked again. "The next time a team member approaches you and asks for advice, take a deep breath and think about the drama triangle. Instead of giving advice, first try to help your team member find the answer to the question. Use Socrates' midwife technique. This way you are also helping, but you are more helpful than if you just helped by giving advice. The beauty of this is also that you show your team members that you trust in them to come up with the right solutions, and that you want them to make decisions themselves. You educate your organization in the sense that more and more team members take ownership of their tasks, projects, and—most importantly—the results they achieve. They become leaders themselves. You create a culture of ownership, you empower your team members, and you create accountability. Which brings us to the final two effective leadership house pillars: accountability and empowerment." Sophia offered Felix her lipstick and, without being prompted, Felix wrote 'Accountability' inside a rectangle next to 'Joint Plans' and 'Empowerment' inside a rectangle next to 'Accountability'.

Felix returned the lipstick and said, "'Empowerment' and 'Accountability', again two—"

"Don't say *buzzwords*, Felix," she said with a bit of a cautionary smile.

"*Interesting* words, then?" Felix said, grinning mischievously. "I'm curious to hear how holding team members accountable actually fits into the leadership foundation. You said I should trust my team members. How can I trust them and hold them accountable at the same time?"

"Actually, trust and accountability reinforce each other. Let us explore why."

CHAPTER 9

LOSING CONTROL

"Treat a man as he is, and he will remain as he is. Treat a man as he can and should be, and he will become as he can and should be."

—Stephen R. Covey

"So, you wondered how you can trust team members while holding them accountable at the same time? Good question, Felix. In fact, this is one of the first questions people ask when I talk about the accountability concept in the context of The Leadership House framework. Let me tell you this: trust and accountability are not mutually exclusive. They reinforce one another. But before we get there, what is the difference between responsibility and accountability? Do you know?"

"People are responsible for specific teams, projects, and departments, no? Like our CTO. Tim is responsible for our tech infrastructure. He's responsible for the development of products and product features. Or our VP of Sales and Customer Success, Steve, is in charge of—surprise, surprise—our customers. He has revenue targets and must ensure the customer is happy."

"What about you, Felix? What are you responsible for?"

"As the CEO, I am responsible for the success of the company in general."

"Well, you are not wrong. But when coaching leaders, I like to quote Simon Sinek. He said, 'Leadership is not about being in charge. Leadership is about taking care of those in *your* charge.' As a leader, you are responsible for and in charge of the people who are responsible for the success of your business. For instance, Steve is in charge of the sales and customer success teams who are in charge of the customer. Tim, your CTO, is responsible for the tech team who is responsible for developing products and product features as well as ensuring your tech infrastructure is stable, secure, and scalable. And you, Felix, you are responsible for your leadership team. As a leader, you are responsible for and in charge of people."

"Did you just say you also work as a coach?"

"Yes, somewhat. After I went through my leadership coaching, my coach told me I was ready to go out and help others, too. Since then, I have coached startup founders, senior executives, and people who had been promoted into leadership positions. They all wanted to become better leaders and did not know how to approach that goal. I have been doing this despite being the CEO of Sand Enterprises. Coaching people and seeing how they improve their leadership skills and become more self-confident in their leadership positions is strongly rewarding."

"This explains a lot. It's like I won a free leadership coaching session by getting stuck in this elevator with you. Thanks!"

Sophia laughed. "You are welcome, Felix. I can hear and see how tough your leadership journey has been so far. Many challenges and a lot of frustration. Not to mention your fights with your investor. But be sure that all leaders are always a work in progress. Unfortunately, your leadership path will never end— there is no finish line. But your path does not have to be so burdensome. You are very curious and a fast learner. I am convinced you can become an effective leader. A coach could definitely help you on your leadership path. If you are willing to improve and are open to coaching, you will notice improvement every day."

"If I take on my next role or build my next company, would you become my coach?"

"Let us discuss this when the time comes," she said. "You are still the CEO of DGTLY. Let us go back to responsibility and accountability. So—we can conclude that responsibility means you take ownership of a job, a task, a project, or people. What does accountability mean then?"

"Hmm," Felix thought. "I mean, I know that I must hold people accountable. Which means... um... that I make sure my folks do what they're supposed to do?"

"First of all, let me stress that many of my coachees cannot immediately explain the difference between responsibility and accountability. You are not alone. Very often, *responsibility* and *accountability* are used interchangeably, or the answers get blurry."

"So accountability doesn't mean to ensure that people do what they're responsible for?"

"No. That would mean that you control your team members. Controlling team members is an outdated leadership style. It was applied by leaders who led with the mindset of 'command and control'. They told team members what to do and controlled whether those team members indeed followed through."

"Okay."

"If you controlled your people, would this be an effective use of your time?"

"Probably not."

"No, it would not. And what about your team members? Would they like this relationship, being controlled by you?"

"I guess not. I guess they would feel micromanaged."

"Indeed, they would. The 'command and control' leadership style worked in a world where employees had to handle physical tasks, in a world where you could say and define exactly what everybody was supposed to do. Think of an assembly line worker. You would tell him or her what to do and ensure they did exactly what they had been told. This does not work anymore. Today, we live and work in a world where you want to tap into the knowledge and experience of your team members. You pay your people for their knowledge and experience. You pay them so they tell *you* what to do."

"That's what Steve Jobs once said, right? 'It doesn't make sense to hire smart people and then tell them what to do. We hire smart people so they can tell *us* what to do'."

"Indeed," she smiled. "But let us go back to accountability. An effective leadership style that works in today's world requires you to involve your team members in the goal-setting process. You do not tell them what goals they have to achieve. You invite them to the process. Then, you create joint plans and allocate clear responsibilities so everybody knows what they are in charge of. Let us recap: responsibility means that one takes ownership of a specific task, project, or team. Accountability goes a step further. If team members are accountable, they take ownership of both the tasks *and* the results achieved. Let me say that again: they take ownership of both tasks *and* the results achieved. That is accountability—or at least accountability as I define it."

"They take ownership of tasks *and* the results achieved," Felix repeated.

"Yes. At the end of the day, only results matter. As a leader, you do not care about tasks completed. What matters are the results. In an organization where people are only allocated responsibilities, you hear things like 'Task completed!', 'I have done my job', 'It is not my fault that we did not achieve our goals', and 'This is not my responsibility'. In contrast, in an organization determined by a culture of accountability, people understand that they are measured by the results they achieve. What does this change, Felix?"

"If they see that they're not achieving their goals, they'll try different things? They ask others for help?"

"Yes, and it changes their behavior even *before* they embark on a new project. If team members know that they are measured by results only, they check whether they have everything they need beforehand. And they check whether they need input from other team members or teams and invite them to the process. And they do not ask for help only if they notice the team might fail. They also offer help if they notice that shared goals cannot be achieved because one team member is struggling. Isn't this nice?"

"It is. It sounds so easy. What happens if a team might fail because one team member underperforms? Remember the developer I told you about? She was constantly underperforming and holding back the team."

"In an environment where accountability prevails, you may already see that underperformers change for the better. But other team members, especially peers, call out bad behavior. If they notice they are failing because others are not providing their deliverables in time, they speak up. They encourage team members and also offer help. But they also call out bad behavior if others do not live up to team standards and shared values. If the team culture is determined by trust, that is no issue. A CTO I once worked with put it this way: 'We play the ball, not the player.'"

"Interesting. I like that. 'We play the ball, and not the player.'"

"Me, too. Believe me, accountability creates totally different team dynamics. *Healthy* team dynamics. And you see, trust and accountability reinforce one another. The higher the trust in the team, the easier it is to hold people accountable. And there is one additional and very important performance driver stemming from a culture determined by accountability."

"Which is?"

"You turn followers into leaders."

"How is that?"

"Think about a middle manager who is used to only being responsible. She was once used to doing her job, but now she has to take ownership of the result. It is not enough that she liaises with other team members and teams before she starts to work on a project. It is not enough that she offers help. If she truly buys into the accountability concept, she will not only delegate tasks to the team members she is leading, but she will also measure these team members by the results they achieve. If done correctly, the accountability concept trickles down through an organization and turns more and more followers into leaders. Then magic happens. And at some point, you have created an organization of leaders. Intriguing, no?"

"I like it."

"Let me test you on this one, Felix. Can you delegate responsibilities?"

"Sure. That's what I do day in and day out."

"Right. Can you delegate accountability?"

"Hmm. Can I delegate the ownership of results? No, I don't think so."

"Correct. You can delegate responsibility, but you cannot delegate accountability. And this is also why you as the founder and leader are always— and forever will be—ultimately accountable for the results DGTLY achieves. No finger pointing, no blame game. You are the founder and CEO of DGTLY. You are the leader of this company. And whatever goes wrong, you are accountable for it. You have decided to hire your team. You can delegate responsibilities to the team, and you can create a culture of accountability in which your team members take ownership of tasks and results. But if your team fails, you are accountable."

"And what about the shareholders, the board, the investors?"

"You are the one who created an organization having all these stakeholders," Sophia reminded him. "Was not this also your leadership decision?"

"Leadership debt, I guess."

"Yes, to a certain extent. Take your investor as an example. You decided to accept Peter's money. It was your job to analyze whether you could work well with him and whether Peter is a team player. If I recall correctly, you had other offers on the table and decided to go with Peter because of the valuation only. Right?"

"Unfortunately, yes."

"If you are not content with your investor, sorry—but that falls upon you. All startup failures can be attributed to bad decisions the founders make."

"So then Peter is right if he says it's all my fault."

"Water under the bridge, Felix. As long as we learn from our past mistakes, all will be well. There is not more we can do than to live in the here-and-now while also looking ahead."

"Wise words."

Sophia smiled. "If you had to create a new and realistic plan for DGTLY, is there anything to remember in terms of responsibility and accountability?"

"Sure. I'd try to allocate clear responsibilities and hold my team accountable. I'd let them assume ownership of the results. Right?"

"Right, Felix. Very good. Now, we have talked about accountability. But there is one last pillar we have not yet talked about. And that is the pillar of 'Empowerment'." Sophia pointed to the elevator wall and the last pillar of The Leadership House. "What does empowerment mean and why is it important?"

"Sorry, Sophia, but this is another one of those buzzwords."

"Agreed. There are many buzzwords when you talk about leadership. *Trust*, *accountability*, *empowerment*. It is one of the main reasons why the leadership concept itself is so intangible for so many leaders. Give it a try! What does empowerment mean?"

"I give them power? Like, what we've just discussed before? I get less involved and let my team decide how they'll deliver on the plans? I make sure they've got all they need? And I find the correct spot on the leadership scale?"

"Not bad, Felix, not bad. Indeed, the concept of accountability will only bear fruit if it is accompanied by empowerment. If your team members are to own both the tasks and their results, they must have all they need and must also be entitled to make the respective decisions. Or, conversely, you cannot ask your team members to own the results without also giving them ownership of what they do. This is where the rubber meets the road. And yes, you will probably choose to sit at the lower end of the leadership scale and be less involved in the *how*."

"To be honest, Sophia, whenever I try to avoid any kind of micromanagement and let my teams be, it always feels uncomfortable. It feels as if I'm losing control. We touched on this before. But losing control is not easy."

"I understand. Again, you are not alone in this. Many of the people I coach have had the same uncomfortable feeling. But you do not have to feel uncomfortable losing control. In fact, you should celebrate it—as long as you follow The Leadership House framework. Effective leaders craft an inspiring vision, create an environment of trust and accountability, move the leadership scale up and down with ease, and empower their teams. If the team pursues shared goals and joint plans on the basis of shared values, the teams will magically cooperate and work towards your vision. And they will love to work for a leader like you."

"Sounds pretty good to me."

Sophia smiled. "It certainly should. And do not forget, you retain the decision-making power for the most important decisions and can concentrate your remaining time on your people."

"Pretty wise, I must say."

"The leadership guide I told you about contains a clear definition of effective leadership. Do you want to hear it?"

"Do you even have to ask?" he laughed.

"Good then. Here is what leading effectively truly is: on the basis of trust, accountability, and shared values, empowering a strong team to execute joint plans towards shared goals and an inspiring vision."

"That encompasses all Leadership House pillars and its foundation."

"Yes."

"Someday, *you* should be talking at one of the events here," Felix smiled, though he was utterly serious. "If you like, I can introduce you to the incubator CEO. Nice guy. I'm sure he'd love to have you as a keynote speaker or guest. And all startups would love to learn about The Leadership House concept. It would have helped *me* if we'd met earlier, that's for sure."

"That is really nice of you, Felix." Then Sophia looked at her watch. "We have been in this elevator for an hour and a half now. I would say they could get this beast going again."

"Agreed. And thanks, Sophia—I'd almost forgotten that we're stuck in this medieval torture chamber."

"Oh, I am sorry, Felix—I had forgotten all about your claustrophobia. But it looked to me as though you handled it just fine."

"You know what? I did. Our conversation helped a lot. But I agree that it would be great if they freed us now. But hey—not before you've told me about the roof."

"The roof?"

"Every house has a roof, doesn't it? What about the roof of The Leadership House?"

Sophia laughed. "You are really quite naturally curious, Felix. And an eager learner. I like that. Okay then. The roof."

CHAPTER 10

THERE IS NO TRYING

"Action without vision is only passing time, vision without action is merely daydreaming, but vision with action can change the world."

—Nelson Mandela

"Felix, as you love the Tarantino movie *Pulp Fiction*, you probably remember what Samuel L. Jackson's character, Jules the gangster, says in the film. What he says about the path of the righteous man. Do you remember?"

"Sure. I've watched the movie so many times I know many of the best quotes by heart. He said, 'The path of the righteous man is beset on all sides by the iniquities of the selfish and the tyranny of the evil men—"

"Stop right there!" Sophia interrupted. "Now, exchange 'the righteous man' with 'the leader' and leave out 'the tyranny of the evil men'. What remains?"

"The path of *the leader* is beset on all sides by the inequities of the selfish."

"Correct. I recently watched the movie again. And when Samuel L. Jackson quoted the *Bible*, I immediately noticed this. If you exchange the words as you have just done, it says a lot about the leadership path."

"The leadership path is beset on all sides by the inequities of the selfish?"

"Yes. Being a leader is difficult. There are many, many leadership challenges waiting for you everywhere. If you want to become a highly effective leader, you must overcome your leadership challenges and ensure you execute your plans. So then, it is 'Execution' that you can write into a roof that you can draw above The Leadership House pillars."

"I don't know about this... my artwork isn't nearly as good as yours," Felix joked.

"Come on now!" Sophia replied with a smile. "Just draw it and write it!"

"That sounds like 'command and control' to me!" Felix said, feigning indignancy. "I'm kidding, obviously. Hand me your lipstick."

Felix did what he was told and drew a triangle above The Leadership House pillars, wrote the word 'Execution' inside it, and handed back the lipstick.

"You know, Felix, leadership is no different than business in general. Strategy is nice. Theory is helpful. But what matters most is execution. I have worked with many founders and executives over the years, and I can say that it is execution that differentiates the great from the good. Execution, execution, execution. That is what counts."

"Well, if I'm honest with myself, I must confess I didn't ensure we executed our plans. And you know something? I've always thought I was a good leader.

I mean, I've honestly always thought I've done a decent job as a leader. But after our conversation, I must confess I've screwed it up. I'm a complete mess when it comes to leadership. I've learned a lot from you in this short while. But will I really be able to make the leap from founder to leader? I'm not sure. I mean, you know so much more than I do."

"Do not be so tough on yourself, Felix. As I have said many times already, you are not alone. I have coached many leaders who pretended to be self-confident, when in reality they were full of self-doubts. Having self-doubts is one of the biggest leadership challenges. And almost all the people I coach face this leadership challenge as well. They think they cannot do it. They have difficulties trusting their team members. They feel uncomfortable losing control. They think they cannot succeed. They fear that their decisions are wrong. They do not know how to deal with conflicts. They do not know how to handle pressure. They have moments when they want to give up. They all doubt their leadership skills."

"Yes. That definitely sounds familiar," Felix sighed.

"Do not give up, Felix. Press on," Sophia urged. "Overcome your challenges and ensure you and your team execute your plans. There are tools that can help you succeed. Like The Leadership House framework. There are coaches who can help you succeed. Ask for help and hire one. A coach can help you walk the leadership path and overcome all leadership challenges successfully."

"Okay," Felix said confidently. "I won't give up."

"Great. As I said, press on."

"Sophia, you have just named so many challenges leaders have to overcome. What, in your experience, is the biggest challenge?"

"I think there is no *one biggest challenge*. Although, I think all leaders have self-doubts from time to time. And many leaders I have worked with had difficulties finding the right balance between being hands-on and hands-off. You know, in the sense of not having been able to smoothly navigate the leadership altitudes we talked about. Or moving up and down the leadership scale with ease. But, then again, we are all different and face different challenges."

"Okay. I understand."

"When I asked you to change the *Pulp Fiction* quote, did you notice I did not ask you to delete 'by the inequities of the selfish', too? So that then the quote would instead be, 'The leadership path is beset on all sides'."

"Actually, no. I thought 'The leadership path is beset on all sides by the inequities of the selfish' was just closer to what Samuel L. Jackson's character actually says."

"No, Felix. I deliberately kept it that way. Another big challenge many leaders face is creating teamwork and a set of individuals who let their egos take a backseat. In fact, many people in business prioritize their own interests over the interests of the team. Never—and I really mean never—accept your team members putting themselves first. Whether it is a shareholder, a board member, a colleague, or a partner, you must ensure everybody puts the *team* first. It is all about teamwork. The beauty of putting the team first is that if the team wins, then all team members win, too. But you already know how to create teamwork, right?"

"Right. Now I do. But there are also circumstances I cannot influence. Like the current macroeconomic climate. High inflation, rising interest rates, and our small business clients' unwillingness to invest in digital tools."

"True. In terms of challenges, there are and always will be external challenges that you will have to cope with. Competition, a macroeconomic crisis, a pandemic—the list goes on. If you face external challenges, remember that the only things we are in complete control of are our judgments, decisions, and actions. Everything else depends, at least to some extent, on external circumstances we cannot influence. That is the dichotomy of control."

"The dichotomy of control?" Felix repeated.

"Yes, your job as a leader is to spend your energy on things and circumstances you can change and to make the best out of each situation. Felix, you should embrace these external circumstances for what they are: obstacles to overcome."

"Sometimes that's easier said than done."

"I agree," Sophia said. "But what you can impact and what you can change is the internal organization. You can change how your organization copes with external challenges. You can impact your team and you can impact the culture in your team. If you apply what we have discussed today, if you apply The Leadership House framework, you can prepare your organization for the external and internal challenges ahead. But most importantly...," Sophia paused. "But most importantly, you can change *yourself*. You can work on your leadership style. And you can develop strong leadership skills. And eventually, you will be a highly effective leader that leads with ease. But it takes time. You do not become capable of leading effectively overnight."

"Thanks. That's encouraging. But, as you know, I don't have time. Tomorrow, it's game over."

"Whatever happens tomorrow, it does not mean 'game over'. It is just another day that you can use to become a better leader."

"Okay, will do. I'll definitely try."

"This is the second time you have said you would 'try'. There is no trying, Felix."

Felix smiled. "'There is no trying' isn't from a Tarantino movie. That's Yoda from *Star Wars*."

"Correct. And I like *Star Wars*, too."

"You are really an extraordinary woman."

"Thanks. I will take that as a compliment."

After a few moments of comfortable silence, Felix said to Sophia, "Help!" Then with a smile, he added, "Honestly, Sophia, please help me! Can you please coach me? I mean, you said you've worked with founders before."

"That is right. And I am flattered by your kind request—and compliment. I like you, Felix. Let me suggest the following: instead of attending this startup event, you will go back to your team and jointly work on a strategy on how to solve the issue with your shareholders. There is still time until tomorrow—that is, if we can get out of this elevator any time soon. And next week, you give me a call and we can discuss whether you still need help and, if you do, how we might work together. How does that sound?"

"It sounds amazing. Thank you so much. I won't disappoint you. While it looks like I won't be hearing what this famous investor on the fifth floor has to say, I guess I can cope with that."

"Maybe he has some interesting learnings to share. But now is the time for you to be with your team and solve your problems. If the guy is still speaking up there and shares something you should know, I will let you know later on. Okay?"

"Absolutely. And I'll try—*whoops*, sorry! I mean, I won't disappoint you."

"I dare you, Felix," Sophia said, firing him another wink.

Suddenly, the elevator rumbled and dropped a few inches. Scared, Felix looked into Sophia's eyes; she also appeared a bit concerned. But then the elevator slowly began to move. Felix and Sophia stood up and nervously watched the numbers in the display above the elevator door. *3, 4, 5...* They both sighed, relieved, and the doors slowly opened, screeching the same loud, mechanical sound as when they first stepped inside. Only this time, they were free.

"Freedom at last," Felix said. In fact, he noticed that he felt freer—freer than ever before. He felt incredible, actually.

"Yes, free at last. Now go and hurry to your team."

Felix nodded and gestured for Sophia to go first. She exited the cabin and together they walked down the hallway. At the end of it were the stairs that Felix would take to get back down to the ground floor.

Sophia turned to Felix and said, "Goodbye, Felix. Good luck, and we will talk soon."

"Goodbye, Sophia. And thank you so much already. I'll let you know how everything turns out. How can I get in touch with you?"

"Connect with me on *LinkedIn*," she smiled. And with that, she turned and opened the door in front of her. Just as she did, a loud voice over a microphone shouted, "Aha, and there she is—finally! Please, everybody, please welcome Sophia van de Sand, CEO of Sand Enterprises. Mentor, coach, successful business angel, and our unicorn hunter who will talk to us about leadership and growth today!" The applause was almost deafening.

Sophia stopped, turned around, and smiled again at Felix.

"C'mon, now. Sophia? *You're* 'the guy'?" he shouted. On the one hand, he couldn't believe it. On the other hand, it made perfect, perfect sense.

"Correct, Felix. I am 'the guy'. Uma Thurman is going to be speaking tonight. And do not worry—you have already heard my speech anyway. In fact, you had a front-row seat. But hurry now. Your team needs you."

"Aye, aye. I'll be gone faster than you can say 'blueberry pie'," Felix replied, referencing another quote from *Pulp Fiction*.

"'Blueberry pie," Sophia said with a grin.

***

Felix ran down the stairs. When he got outside the building, he took out his phone and called Mark. Felix was glad when he picked up.

"Felix, where—"

"No time to talk, Mark. I'll explain everything to you later. Please call everybody from our team. We'll meet in thirty minutes in our office to discuss how we're going to turn this ship around."

Before Mark could say anything, Felix hung up and ran back to the office.

CHAPTER 11

HIGH NOON

"Changing an organization, a company, a country—or a world—begins with
the simple step of changing yourself."

—Tony Robbins

I t was five minutes to noon on the following day. All the board members sat around the table in the DGTLY conference room. Nobody had said a word yet, save for a brief 'hi' or 'hello'. Felix could feel the tension in the air and thought, "This is a bit like the opening scene in Sergio Leone's epic western film *Once Upon A Time In The West*. This is definitely not going to be a standard board meeting."

Normally when the board convened, Felix and Mark sat at one long side of the table, and Douglas and Peter usually sat opposite them. Today, Felix had taken a seat at the head side of the table, leaving Mark to his left and the other two to the right. He thought that this new seating arrangement might create an atmosphere less oppressive than the usual board meeting atmosphere. Instead of two opposing parties who talk *at* each other, like those in the British Parliament seem to prefer, he wanted one team to work together on solving the problems the company was facing. Felix wanted to talk *with* the other board members.

He looked at Mark and noticed him nervously swaying back and forth in his chair. "We've come quite far together," Felix thought to himself, before looking into Mark's eyes as if to reassuringly say, "Calm down. It'll be okay."

Suddenly, Peter interrupted the silence. "We're all here, Felix." His tone was one of boredom and annoyance. "Can we please start? I've got a hard stop at two o'clock. We all know what today's meeting is about."

"Sure, Peter," Felix said. "It's high noon anyway." Nobody laughed. "So, let's kick off. Hi, everybody. I'm welcoming you to our extraordinary board meeting that Peter had asked me to convene yesterday. The agenda for today's meeting reads as follows—"

"We know the agenda," Peter interrupted. "I suggest we skip the opening words and the usual business update stuff and jump directly to the main agenda point. Your removal from office. Okay?"

"Sorry, Peter, but before that, please allow me to follow the agenda and say a few opening words."

"Ahh, Felix, spare us. You're done. Your time is up."

Douglas jumped in and said, "Please, Peter—not so fast. I would actually like to hear what Felix has to say."

"For God's sake. So be it," Peter muttered.

"Thanks, Douglas. Much appreciated." Felix stood up, pushed his chair towards the table and said, "This won't take long. And as soon as I've finished, you can remove me from office."

Douglas nodded as if to say, "Good, let's get on with it then!"

"Yesterday, Peter called me and informed me that you two, Douglas and Peter, had decided I was not the right person to lead DGTLY anymore. Like always, Peter said I'd been a bad leader and that I'd failed miserably. Also, like always, I did not agree with his assessment. I thought it was completely unfair. I referred to the many external challenges we have been facing, like the pandemic and how it has impacted our customers. And I referred to our internal challenges, like our key hires who had not been living up to our expectations. I blamed our Chief Revenue Officer for having left so quickly. I blamed our UK country head for not having pulled it off. And I accused Peter of having forced us into this situation with his, 'You need to grow, grow, grow' remarks."

"And?" Peter asked.

"And I was wrong, Peter. I was wrong. From now on, no more excuses. I've already come to understand that there is no one to blame for our situation except for me. I agree with you, Peter—I've failed as a leader. But I'll change. In fact, I've already changed. You've got a new Felix in front of you. You've got a Felix in front of you who accepts full responsibility for our company, our people, and the results we've achieved and *will* achieve. I accept full accountability."

Peter groaned. "Too late, Felix. Your time is up."

"Please, Peter, bear with me. Yesterday, I assembled the complete leadership team. We started at eight p.m. and finished this morning. Steve was the last person. He left around ten. We spent the whole night together discussing what we've got to do to turn this ship around. We discussed in an absolute transparent and honest manner what we must do now to achieve our vision. What must we do now to create a business that generates one hundred million in revenue? We could agree on the following four to-dos—"

"Please!" Peter groaned again.

Felix ignored him. "We agreed on four to-dos. Please, consider these to-dos as suggestions that I want to discuss with you."

"Go ahead!" Douglas said.

"To-do number one: we agreed we must create a culture determined by trust. We must create trust in the leadership team. So far, I've trusted nobody but Mark. And I learned yesterday that nobody in the leadership team has trusted me. This will change. I will ensure we create an environment in which everybody feels safe to speak up, disagree, and challenge one another. This especially includes me. I need people around me who are at ease with challenging me. But it's not just in the leadership team where we must create trust. We must also build trusting relationships among us board members. All board members are supposed to create value for our company. But you, Peter and Douglas, can only do so if you have all the relevant information and if you trust in me. I admit that I haven't been transparent with you. I haven't been transparent with you because I feared if you knew what was going on in our organization, you would remove me from office. But here I am. I may be removed from office anyway."

"You will, Felix. You will," Peter said.

Douglas intervened, "Please, Peter, let Felix continue."

"I haven't been able to create trust in the leadership team. And I haven't created trust in the board. It's clear to me now. Absolutely clear. If there's no trust and no constructive discussions, then there's no success. Yesterday, I promised my team they could trust me and that I would trust them. The reaction from the team was only positive. It was the first time since long ago that there was excitement in the room. I sensed how happy everybody was. And I noticed how desperately everybody had been longing for a change. I hereby invite you to participate in this change. From now on, I'll trust you. And I promise you that you can trust me. I won't disappoint you anymore."

He panned the room slowly as he spoke, examining everyone's faces. Douglas was listening attentively. On Peter's face, there was boredom, frustration, and impatience. Unfazed, Felix continued.

"What else?" Peter asked demandingly.

"To-do number two: the team. We also agreed we must rebuild the leadership team. We need the best people in the right positions. And, for this, we have to make a few changes."

Peter raised an eyebrow, but Felix continued. "Last night, we came up with the following changes. Mark steps down as Chief Operating Officer. In our meeting, I asked him to share with the team what he thought about his performance and whether he thought he was a good COO. Much to the surprise of everyone in the room, Mark replied that he believed he was a good sparring partner and a very good co-founder, but that there were probably better COOs out there, people who could better help me and the team. It's very tough for me to say this, but I agreed with his assessment. As I said, Mark therefore offered to step down as COO. He'll remain in the role until we've hired someone new. And he'll leave the operational business completely as soon as he's found a new role in a new company." Felix looked at Mark and asked, "Mark, do you want to add anything?"

"Thanks, Felix." Mark looked at Peter and Douglas. "Guys, I believe I am a very good founder and am able to build companies. But I have realized I am not passionate about growing businesses further and further, and probably also lack the required skills. I am going to build a new venture or join another early-stage startup founder team. We'll see. As for DGTLY, I'll remain a board member and will do my very best to contribute even more to our board discussions. Thank you." He nodded to Felix.

"Thanks, Mark. I told you this already yesterday, but let me say it again: I'm proud of you and your decision. Without you, we wouldn't be here."

You could hear a pin drop in the room now. Felix looked at Douglas and Peter, but he couldn't tell what they were thinking.

"There are two more changes in the leadership team we would like to suggest," Felix continued. "Firstly, we would like to hire a Chief People Officer who helps me—no, sorry. Who helps *us* hire the right talent, put that talent into the right seats, and ensure all team members embrace a teamwork mentality. We need someone who knows how to create a culture in which all employees thrive and enjoy working. We need someone who creates a culture determined by trust, accountability, and collaboration. For this, we need help from an experienced Chief People Officer. I can't do this on my own.

With regard to both new hires, the COO and the Chief People Officer, we'll be looking for the best candidates, but we prefer female hires with diverse backgrounds. Our team is not diverse at all. We must change this. And we must change this fast."

Felix looked closely at the other board members' faces again but still couldn't identify any sort of reaction. It was as if Douglas and Peter had been frozen. Undaunted, he continued.

"Secondly, we do not want to continue our search for a new Chief Revenue Officer. We do not believe that a new CRO solves our problems. In fact, we don't have a problem a CRO could solve. Our problem is that we've not yet generated product/market fit in our expansion markets and with regard to some of our products. We must focus on solving *this* problem. And our product and tech teams can solve this problem with the help of our marketing, sales, customer success, and finance teams. Instead of hiring a CRO, we want to promote Mick and Steve into C-level positions again. They have strong functional knowledge and good leadership skills. And they've proven they can work as a team. We trust in their ability to grow the business. If you agree, they'll become Chief Marketing Officer and Chief Sales and Customer Success Officer once again."

Peter scoffed a little. Then he asked, "Do you think they can also sell successfully into the enterprise customer segment, Felix? Selling to large corporations is a completely different animal. It requires a different go-to-market strategy. Different marketing material. And different salespeople. Salespeople who know how to sell to enterprise clients. Sales cycles are longer. Not to mention customer success. Enterprise customers expect a totally different service."

"Good point, Peter. And before I answer your question, let me stress that these are exactly the discussions we should have had earlier in the board. And these are exactly the discussions we'll be having going forward. To answer your question, we agreed—and this is our third to-do—that we change our strategy and focus again on selling to small- and medium-sized business customers. If product and tech teams focus on these customer segments, we'll get to product/market fit faster. Our marketing and sales teams know how to sell to these customers. And our customer success people know how to service them. We suggest we stop selling to enterprise clients, at least for the time being and until we have grown our business successfully in our core customer segments and all our expansion markets." Felix paused. "Any questions from anyone with regard to this new strategy?"

Douglas said, "I think we have to think about this a bit. We might ask for some more details. Peter?"

Peter nodded.

"Fully understood, guys. So, let me continue then. If we want to change our strategy, we also need to change our business plan and our financial model. It's demotivating that we miss our targets month after month." Felix reached for a pile of paper in front of him and handed five sheets each to Peter and Douglas. "Consider the plan you see there on paper a work in progress and only a first draft. But based on the input every team member gave yesterday, we believe we can get to one hundred million in revenue in five years if we achieve all of the five shared goals mentioned in the documents."

"I need more time to review this, Felix," Peter said. "This is something the board needs to be provided with way in advance of the meeting."

"I agree. Going forward, you'll receive all relevant information at least five business days in advance. We'll also change what we're discussing in the board meetings. I suggest we provide you with all relevant financial information in the board pack that you get in advance of the meetings. In those meetings, we'll then answer your respective questions and focus the rest of the time on the three to five most important topics we've got amongst the leadership team. By doing so, we'll make our board meetings more effective. And we can tap into your knowledge and experience. As for the new plan, I suggest we have another meeting next week in which we can discuss our shared goals and our joint plan with you."

"Go on, Felix. You said you had four to-dos," Peter prodded.

"The fourth to-do concerns the board composition. I would like to add an independent board member. I would like to add someone who acts as a board member providing us with fresh perspectives and willing to coach the leadership team. I've already identified someone. Her name is Sophia van de Sand."

"I met her last night at the incubator event," Douglas said. "She was very impressive, I must admit. And you know her, Felix?"

"Yes, I had a free coaching session with her, and that session changed everything completely. Without that session, you'd be sitting here with the old Felix. I would like to ask her—with your permission—if she wants to join our board and coach our leadership team."

"And change the voting rights?" Peter asked, concerned.

"No. I want her to add value to our discussions. Sophia will certainly have to be paid. And she will certainly also have to get some stock options. But I want to leave the board rights as they are. If you, as my major shareholders, do not believe in me and my ability to lead this business, I'll resign voluntarily."

Then Felix paused, took a deep breath, and said, "I know that you've come here to remove me from office. If you're still thinking this is the best for our company, please let me know and I'll resign. But if there's a modicum of hope left that I might be the right person to pull it off, please give me this last chance. I won't disappoint you again. Trust me."

"Thank you, Felix," Douglas said. "Can you give Peter and me a few minutes to discuss this between the two of us? Would this be okay for you?"

"Absolutely. Mark, let's go."

Mark stood up and they both left the room, Felix shutting the door behind them. They walked over to the hangout area around the corner, sat down in the large plastic bean bags, and waited.

"What do you think?" Mark asked.

"I don't know," Felix replied, a bit nervous. "I guess it all depends on how Douglas sees the situation. We've done all we can. I've made many mistakes. But I hope I get a last chance. At least I've never been more motivated to become a better leader! And I want this company to succeed. We'll see, won't we? But I could use a coffee. What about you?"

"I could use a beer," Mark replied with a smile, "but a coffee will do the trick until we know more. I'll go and get us one."

Soon after, Mark and Felix drank their coffees without any further exchange. Both were exhausted.

It took Peter and Douglas about thirty minutes to reach a decision. At one forty-five, Douglas stuck his head into the hangout area and asked Felix and Mark to return.

Once the door was closed and everyone was seated again, Douglas said, "Felix, while Peter and I do not find common ground very often, we both agree that the last year was far from satisfactory. I have been disappointed. As a business angel, I take a lot of risk when I decide to invest in a founder. And the least I can expect from a founder is honesty and transparency. I wanted to trust you, but over time I lost that trust. And I lost faith in you, as well. I did not believe any longer that you were the right person to lead our business. However, I must confess I am impressed by what you have just told us. Not only is this the first time since Peter invested that I have seen a somewhat realistic plan, but I am also seeing a founder who is self-aware and willing to change. Felix, I could convince Peter to give you one last chance. I trust you will walk the talk now. I expect absolute transparency and honesty. In return, please do not hesitate to reach out to us. We are here to help. Our interests are still aligned. Do not forget this."

Turning his head to Mark, he continued, "For you, Mark, I have utmost respect. The decision to step down is a brave one. We'll be counting on you when it comes to contributing as a board member to the success of the business. Please actively engage in our board discussions. I wish you all the best for your job search. If you need an intro or would like me to be a reference, just ask. I will happily assist wherever I can. And before I forget, we are fine with Sophia joining the board. But certainly, you will understand that we have to talk with her personally first. Now, I suggest we close this board meeting without any official decisions. And you guys might want to have a nap. After a bit of rest, you'll have a lot to do and a lot to change. Onwards and upwards!"

"Thank you, Douglas. And thank you, Peter," Felix replied, incredibly relieved. "Thank you for the trust and for the last chance. You can count on me." He faced the room. "And with that, I'm closing today's board meeting. I'll send you an invite for another meeting next week. Thank you, everyone—have a great day."

It had become a great day indeed.

THREE YEARS LATER

"The function of leadership is to produce more leaders, not more followers."

—Ralph Nader

It was seven in the evening when Felix passed the lounge corner and the coffee bar on the ground floor of the DGTLY office tower. He strolled confidently to the elevator and entered when the sleek doors slid open. He pressed the button for the rooftop terrace, but just as the doors were beginning to close...

"Stop, stop—please wait!" That female voice was familiar. Felix held his hand between the elevator doors, and when they opened again, there she was—Sophia. She smiled and joined him inside.

"Oh, no. Please, Sophia—not this again!" Felix joked.

"How high is the probability of this happening twice?" Sophia laughed. "And these high-tech elevators rarely get stuck. Hey—since when do you take elevators?"

"Long story," he said as the doors closed. "I went to therapy for my claustrophobia. I'm fine now. I'll never fall in love with elevators, though."

"Ha—I can believe that."

The elevator quickly ascended, reached the rooftop terrace, and the doors slid open. The party had not yet begun, but the band playing that evening was already set to get started. Loud, ambient, chillout music greeted the DGTLY employees, board members, and investors who had already arrived. Gorgeous decorations, lampions, and amazing beach bar furniture made the rooftop terrace a wonderful place to spend the night. It was a fantastic way to celebrate the sale of DGTLY.

"Wonderful," Sophia said, examining the elaborate scene.

Felix replied, "Thanks. We've done our best to make this night special. Wait until the band starts to play. They're great."

A server offered Sophia and Felix a drink. Sophia took a glass of champagne, while Felix opted for a beer.

"By the way, nice dress code," Sophia said. "How did you come up with it?"

"To be honest, I copied it. A cool company in Berlin once gave a party with the same dress code. I'd never heard of 'Bohemian chic' before. But looking around here, I must say it again: it's a great style. Pretty colorful clothing. A bit retro. A bit seventies merged with a bit of hippie, I'd say. I especially like all the natural fabrics."

"How do you like my Boho tunic?" she asked, giving a small twirl.

"It's great, I like this warm blue. Nice hat, also. Can I wear it tonight?"

"No way. Do you know what it is called?"

"How could I know that? Um, beach head? Straw hat?"

"It is called, 'men's boho rock'n'roll straw hat distressed'."

"So, it's a men's hat. Then I *should* wear it."

"Forget it, Felix. You look great without a hat, anyway. A bit like Sunny Crocket from *Miami Vice*." They both laughed.

"Look, there's Mark," Felix pointed out. "Let's join him!" They walked over to Mark, standing alone and sipping a beer. "Can we join you?"

"Sure. Hi, Felix. Hi, Sophia. So—this was it, huh?"

"Sure was. Company sold," Felix replied.

"And for a decent amount of money, might I add," Sophia said.

"Yes, a bit more than two hundred million for a company that generates roughly fifty million in revenue," Mark said. "It could have been more—it only sold for four times the revenue. But we should be fine. I won't complain."

Felix nodded and added, "We didn't build a 'unicorn', but we were on track."

"Agreed," Sophia said. "Actually, it is only because we had been on track to build a unicorn that we found a buyer willing to pay that price."

Felix said, "I've said that before, Sophia. But once again, thanks. Without you, we wouldn't be here tonight."

"No need to thank me."

"*Of course* there's a need to thank you," Mark confirmed. "You've been a great chairman—sorry, chairwoman of the board."

"I am still astonished Peter and Douglas not only offered me a seat at the board table but also the opportunity to chair the board."

Felix replied, "I guess they understood that an independent board member and chairwoman could be better suited for transforming all board members into a team."

"Yes, you may be right," Sophia said, sipping her champagne. "And it was a pleasure to be the chairwoman and help you achieve your goals. Product/market fit in all expansion markets—check. Another thirty million financing round—check. Almost fifty percent revenue growth year on year—check. And, this year, the first enterprise clients—check. It has been one hell of a ride. But quite a successful ride, I must say."

"And with many challenges for me as a leader," Felix admitted. "But not unexpected. You prepared me perfectly for these challenges, Sophia. You've been a wonderful headshrinker."

Sophia laughed. "Your *coach*—not your headshrinker. What about the rest of the leadership team? Will everybody be here tonight, Felix?"

"Steve and Mick won't be able to come tonight. They're with our buyer in Atlanta to discuss the post-merger integration process with regard to the joint go-to-market strategy going forward. But the rest will be here. Tim, Pete, Nick, Ole, and Pamela."

Sophia said, "I am still amazed by how they all developed into leaders. A lot of this leadership development is owed to Pamela. She has done an incredible job as Chief People Officer, don't you think?"

"Agreed. And as the CEO, I was also able to focus more on our people and their development, thanks to Ole. Our Norwegian team member was a super second-in-command and Chief Operating Officer. We've built a strong team, Sophia. Look, there's Peter."

Peter joined them, drink in hand. "Hi, everybody. Great place, Felix. Can't wait to hear the band. But before we party, let me express how happy I am. I haven't made the returns I wanted to make on my investment, but the returns are decent and three years ago I didn't expect to make them. You deserve extra credit, Felix. It was *you* who brought us here. Well done, Felix. Well done!"

"Thanks, Peter. It's appreciated. But as I've learned the hard way, there's no *I* in *team*. We're here because the board acted as a team. We're here because the leadership team acted as a team. We're here because Pamela shaped a company culture of leaders, a culture in which all our employees took ownership of our tasks and results. And we're here because my coach, Sophia, helped me become a better and more effective leader. Without all of her fantastic questions when we were trapped in that elevator three years ago, I would still be looking for many answers. So, no—I don't deserve extra credit. I am just one member of a great team."

Everybody nodded appreciatively, well aware that Felix's modesty was not at all for show.

"What about you, Mark?" Peter asked. "How's your startup doing?"

"We're getting there. We've acquired our first customers and generated our first revenue. I'd say we're all good."

"Good to hear, Mark. Hey—who is that guy over there? I've never seen him before."

"Whom do you mean?" Felix asked.

"That guy across the room. The one with the grey hair. He's probably in his sixties."

"That's my father," Felix said, smiling over at his dad.

"Oh, wow!" Mark said. "I haven't seen him in ages. What did he say when you told him about our exit that pulled in two hundred million?" Mark asked.

"He said he always knew I'd succeed as a founder."

Mark laughed and said, "Sure, he always knew."

"You know him, Mark. He's never been good at admitting he's wrong. But he said one thing that I'll never forget: he said my grandpa would have been proud of me. And that I had the same entrepreneurial spirit he had had."

"That's a nice compliment," Peter replied. "What's next then, Felix?"

"Well, I will remain in office for two more years. That's what I agreed with our buyer. And then, I'm going to do this all over again."

"Another startup?"

"Yep. I'm just loving it. I want to become a serial entrepreneur."

"That's amazing," Peter replied. "Please let me know when the time comes. I'll back you again, provided you accept my money."

"I'll definitely do that, Peter. We had a false start, that's for sure. But we have become a good team."

Felix looked over at Sophia, and this time he was the one offering up a wink. After all, he owed everything to her.

The End

The Leadership House Framework

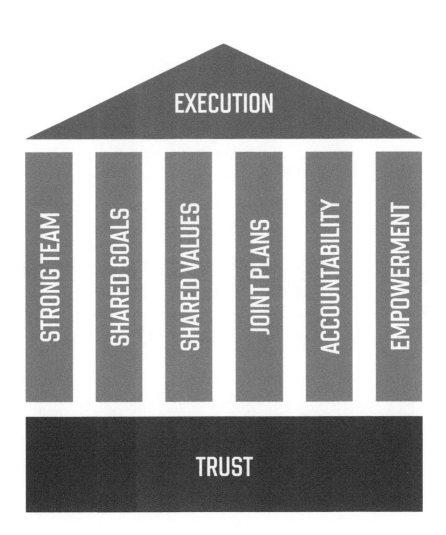

The Leadership Scale

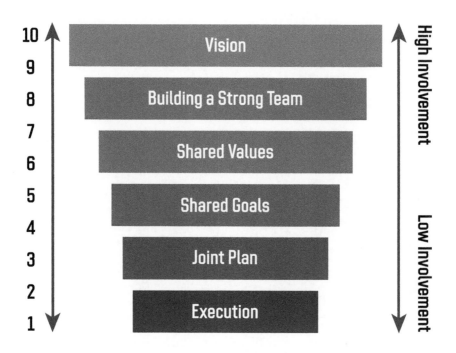

Leadership Coaching & Online Leadership Courses

If you are interested in leadership coaching or online leadership courses, please visit www.patrickflesner.com. Leadership coaching is one of the most effective tools available to take your leadership development to a deeper and more sustainable level. It is the continuous exchange that creates long-lasting results. Leadership coaching can help you as an individual leader, your team, and your entire organization to unlock the full leadership and growth potential.

In the online leadership course, you will not only learn even more about effective leadership. You will also create your own personalized leadership development plan reflecting what you and your teams must do to become an effective leader and a cohesive team that thrives and turns your inspiring vision into reality.

Keynotes

Patrick Flesner delivers both virtual presentations and in-person keynotes about leadership and growth topics.

"Patrick Flesner's keynote at Estonian Business Angels Network investor day during sTARTUp Day was a hit—full of energy and smooth storyline to follow. His passion for leadership was contagious. His ideas to help founders transition to leaders and help leaders improve their leadership skills are pushing leadership thinking.

If you are looking for someone to give a leadership keynote on your event with passion and actionable leadership insights, then I believe Patrick is your man."

—Harri Talin, partner at CIVITTA and co-founder of ChallengerAccelerator.com

If you want Patrick Flesner to keynote your event, please contact him at www.patrickflesner.com.

More about Leadership and Growth

If you are interested in gaining more insight not only about leadership, but also about how to grow businesses successfully, you may enjoy Patrick Flesner's bestselling growth handbook *FastScaling: The Smart Path to Building Massively Valuable Businesses*.

Acknowledgements

Thanks to Rob Peace and Sarah Lewis for copyediting this book. We shared the same vision of creating an outstanding leadership volume, and I could not be more content with your work. You brought the book to a whole new level, and I thank you.

Thanks to Amgad Ibrahim. You have done a great job with regard to the interior design of the first draft version of this book.

I am incredibly proud and grateful that Gisbert Rühl has provided the Foreword to this book and that Howard Behar, Oliver Kaltner, Matthias Heutger, Jörg Jung, and Dr. Carsten Voigtländer have written praise for this book. Thank you!

And, very importantly, I wish to thank my family, especially my wife, Nina, for her understanding and constant support. Without you, I would not have been able to write this book.

I am eternally thankful.

Patrick

Author Bio

Patrick Flesner is a growth capital investor, leadership coach, active keynote speaker, and author. He was a partner at business law firms, a senior executive at METRO Group where he created one of the biggest European venture capital portfolios of companies active in consumer industries and digital commerce, and a partner at the investment firm LeadX Capital Partners. He has been working in private equity, venture capital, and mergers & acquisitions for almost two decades. He has invested in and worked with tech companies throughout the whole of Europe. As an investor, startup board member, coach, and mentor, he has been passing on his actionable leadership and growth insights and leadership development frameworks to founders, entrepreneurs, managers, and leaders across the globe.

His knowledge and experience in the realm of scaling tech businesses have been passionately delivered in his bestselling growth handbook *Fast Scaling: The Smart Path to Building Massively Valuable Businesses*. His leadership expertise is reflected in his leadership story *The Leadership House: A Leadership Tale about the Challenging Path to Becoming an Effective Leader*.

Patrick Flesner's articles about leadership and growth have been published by renowned magazines such as *MIT Sloan Management Review*, *I by IMD*, and *Inc.* magazine. Patrick received a Ph.D. in Law from the University of Cologne and holds a Master of Business Administration (MBA) degree from INSEAD Business School. He lives with his wife and children in Cologne, Germany.